MW01282477

In Search of
William Wolfskill

In Search of
William Wolfskill

JOURNEY TO FIND THE LEGACY

Conchita Thornton Marusich

© Copyright 2017 by Conchita Thornton Marusich
All rights reserved. This book or any portion thereof may not be reproduced in any form or by any electronic or mechanical means or used in any manner whatsoever without the express written permission of the publisher except for the use of brief quotations in a book review or other critical articles that may be written about the book.

Printed in the United States of America.
ISBN-10: 1544624549
ISBN 13: 9781544624549
Library of Congress Control Number: 2017903925
CreateSpace Independent Publishing Platform
North Charleston, South Carolina

Publisher:
Conchita Thornton Marusich
P.O. Box 3005
Napa, California 94558
USA

TABLE OF CONTENTS

ILLUSTRATIONS AND PHOTOGRAPHS

PREFACE

Conchita Thornton Marusich, a descendant of the famous western trapper, trader and trail builder, William Wolfskill, has poured her heart and soul into *In Search of William Wolfskill: Journey to Find the Legacy*. Her book on her legendary great-great-grandfather is a must read for those interested in Western History and the settlement of the West! As the President of the Old Spanish Trail Association, I have traveled the entire trail used by William Wolfskill and his associates as they carved the Old Spanish Trail from the western frontier.

The Old Spanish Trail Association is dedicated to preserving the important history of the Old Spanish Trail for current and future generations. That is why I was excited to read *In Search of William Wolfskill: Journey to Find the Legacy* by my good friend, Conchita Thornton Marusich, which tells the inspiring story of William Wolfskill, a great pioneer and significant historical figure of the West. William and his expedition were explorers who have the distinction of being among the first to blaze the Main Route of the Old Spanish Trail from Abiquiu, New Mexico, to Los Angeles, California, in late 1830 and early 1831. Over time, the Main Route, also known as the Northern Route of the Old Spanish Trail, facilitated trade between New Mexico, Colorado, Utah, Nevada and California from

1829-1848. William Wolfskill, along with thousands of other mountain men, trappers, merchants and traders, overcame unbelievable obstacles during their journeys on the Old Spanish Trail.

This book describes two journeys of exploration. The first story about Conchita Thornton Marusich's great-great-grandfather, will take you back to those Old West days when explorers pushed into new lands and eventually put down roots on the ever-expanding frontier. Wolfskill's adventures will introduce you to this courageous man who was always searching for the next challenge. The second story details Conchita's and her husband, Rich's, 10-year investigation into the William Wolfskill legacy through genealogical and historical research, as well as visits to those places where William traveled, trapped and lived. For Conchita, it was a journey of self-discovery into her family history in order to truly understand firsthand the challenges experienced by her distinguished ancestor.

Conchita's book is engaging and enlightening as you learn about William Wolfskill, trailblazer, adventurer, pioneer, business entrepreneur and civic leader who played a crucial role in the settlement and formation of early Los Angeles.

Ashley Hall
President, Old Spanish Trail Association

ACKNOWLEDGEMENTS

I would like to thank so many people who have helped to make this book possible. First and foremost, I owe the inspiration for this book to my mother, Elena Juarez Wolfskill Thornton, for encouraging me to write about our illustrious ancestor, William Wolfskill. I am also deeply appreciative to my husband, Rich Marusich, who has given me unending support and been my enthusiastic companion during this journey. His sense of humor, feedback and love of the project have been essential over the years. I owe much to my son, Chris, and daughter, Jenny, who both gave me their comments, editing feedback and encouragement. Jenny has been my technical consultant on formatting the book since she is a whiz on the computer. My daughter-in-law, Michelle Del Rosario-Marusich, and son-in-law, Sean Kennedy, helped with their comments and support. Many thanks to Michelle who took my photo for the back cover of the book. I've appreciated the help from my brother, John Thornton and sister-in-law, Maureen Thornton, over the years. A big thank you goes to Joan Hedding, my newly found cousin and descendant from Luis or Lewis Wolfskill, William Wolfskill's youngest son. Her editing skills, knowledge of Wolfskill history, and loan of multiple family photos have been indispensable to this book. I also thank her sister, Michele Stephenson, for her family photos and documents as well as my cousin, Marguerite Oates, who loaned me her mother's papers and letters to Timoteo (Amy Wolfskill Smith Collection). To my cousins, descendants from José or Joseph Wolfskill, William's eldest son and my great-grandfather, I thank Ruth Hoelzel, Marie Terry, Margaret Ann Mahuka, Dona Reusch, Linda Pawinski, Peter Wolfskill Anderson, and my aunt, Victoria Swackenberg, for their encouragement, information and help. And I thank Rich's brother-in-law, W.A. Scott for his help.

A big thank you to my fellow genealogists, Joan Hedding, Pat Geiger, Vickie Thompson, Greg Lowther and Betty Malmgren for their comments and support. I appreciated the early help from Susan Stroh, writing coach; Sondra Farrell, writer; Pat Alexander, historical and educational expert; Gary Fuenfhausen, historian from Arrow Rock, Missouri; Betty Collier, genealogist from Fayette, Missouri; as well as Nancy Pine, writer and teacher. I also thank Andie Reid, from the Early California Population Project, who provided enormous assistance as I searched for baptism, marriage and death documents and Michael Holland, City Archivist at the Los Angeles City Archives. Appreciation goes to many people in the Old Spanish Trail Association (OSTA): Ashley Hall, President of OSTA, who wrote the preface to this book; Alexander King, Director at Large, for his comments and help; Elizabeth Warren, former President of the Nevada Chapter; Al Matheson, former President of the Southern Utah Chapter; Paul Ostapuk, OSTA Secretary; Jack Prichett, President of the Tecopa Chapter; Ruth Friesen, Editor, Spanish Traces; Dr. James Jefferson, Director at Large/Native American; Steve Heath, a former President of OSTA and John Hiscock, OSTA Manager. I would like to thank Richard Salazar who translated documents from the original old Spanish versions into English. I thank Cecelia Peña for her information about the Peña family and the Peña Adobe. I give my appreciation to the Wolfskill Experimental

Farm in Winters, California, and Tony Cristler, the Agricultural Superintendent, for their information about John Reid Wolfskill's farm. Many thanks to the Santa Fe Trail Association (SFTA) and the following members: Joanne VanCoevern, SFTA manager; Alice and David Clapsaddle for their contributions and help; and Jeff Trotman for his guided tour of a section of the Trail. To our good friends in New Mexico, Susan Herrera and Amalio Madueño, I thank them for their hospitality and support during our Taos/Santa Fe research trips. To the park rangers at Black Star Canyon and the Helena Modjeska Historic House and Garden, their information made our trip there very worthwhile. I thank William D. Estrada, Ph.D., Curator, Museum of Natural History of Los Angeles County and Christopher Espinosa, General Manager, El Pueblo de Los Angeles Historical Monument.

My gratitude goes to the Huntington Library; Bancroft Library; UC Irvine Libraries, Special Collections; UC Davis Library, Special Collections; Workman and Temple Family Homestead Museum; the Santa Barbara Mission Archive-Library; the Santa Barbara Trust for Historic Preservation; the California State Library; the LDS Genealogical Family History Library in Salt Lake City, Utah; the Peña Adobe Historical Society; the Vacaville Heritage Council; the Napa Valley College Library and the St. Helena Library. My deep appreciation goes to all the wonderful librarians who helped me find materials and suggested great sources.

I have given thanks to the many people and organizations that helped during our research on my book. If I have forgotten anyone, please know that your assistance was greatly appreciated. It takes a network of generous people and organizations to do extensive research on an historical figure such as William Wolfskill.

CHAPTER 1

JOURNEY TO FIND THE LEGACY

When I started to write about the legacy of my family, I had no idea it would become a journey that consumed my life for 10 years. It all started rather innocently one day, talking to my 88-year-old mother about the fairy tale experience on September 4, 1941, when she was proclaimed the "Queen of the *Pueblo de Los Angeles*." Mama loved to reminisce about her ride in a horse-drawn carriage that took her from the old San Gabriel Mission to downtown Los Angeles. Riding in the "king's coach," Elena Wolfskill led the procession on the nine-mile trek to Olvera Street in commemoration of the founding of Los Angeles by Felipe de Neve in 1781.

"The crowds were wonderful," Mama told me. "We rode down Lincoln Avenue and there were people everywhere. We started the day with a blessing by the priest and ended at the Avila Adobe. That's where I cut a cake celebrating the city's 160th birthday. It was a party I'll never forget." Her eyes sparkled as the memories filled her with nostalgia.

Reminiscing about her day as *"la Reina de Los Angeles,"* Mama sat in her wheelchair, still looking every bit a queen in a bright red beret and matching sweater with a marbled scarf of red and white silk draped around her shoulders. Several strokes had left her unable to walk well but her mind was still razor sharp. I brought out her

Queen Elena Wolfskill Leading Procession to Olvera Street, 1941
Courtesy of Elena Wolfskill Thornton

old scrapbooks filled with yellowing newspaper articles as well as black and white photos. Even though she was legally blind, she could make out shapes and colors seeing the world as if it were an impressionistic painting. I read to her from the old articles describing the procession of men mounted on palomino horses, open carriages and the brightly colored flags of California, Mexico and the Bear Flag Republic fluttering in the wind.

"I remember how handsome Leo Carrillo was that day—every inch a movie star," she said, a smile filling her face.

"And you looked like a star too, Mama," I told her.

Indeed my mother, who was 26 years old when she was crowned Queen of Los Angeles, looked as though she had stepped out of Central Casting, radiant in a white, early-California-style dress made of organdy with a tight bodice and ruffles that cascaded to the ground. A long, white mantilla that had belonged to her grand-mother, Elena de Pedrorena Wolfskill, was draped over her wavy, shoulder-length black hair. But what really stood out was my moth-er's million-dollar smile. It drew people to her then and throughout her life.

"So *hija*," she said, calling me the Spanish word for daughter, "I hope that you will write the story about our family. We don't want our history to fade away. The story of the Wolfskills, the de Pedrorenas and the Lugos is the story about early California. We helped to settle this land and make it what it is."

And so, I made a promise to my mother that I would write about her great-grandfather, William Wolfskill, not realizing that it would take my family and me across the country to Boonesborough, Kentucky, across the Santa Fe Trail, over the Old Spanish Trail to Los Angeles, up to Napa Valley and the city of Winters in California, searching out archives, and tapping into the memories of countless relatives.

My book combines two stories. The first part of every chap-ter is **William's Story**, which recounts William's life. "We are Wolfskills," my mother would say, a sense of honor and duty re-flected in her voice. She would tell us stories about William's his-toric journeys over the Santa Fe Trail and the Old Spanish Trail as well as his importance as the founder of California's commercial citrus industry.

Building on my family history, **William's Story** is also based on extensive research that includes articles written by his son-in-law Henry Dwight Barrows as well as many historical accounts and per-sonal recollections. Another important source is historian Iris Higbie Wilson's landmark book *William Wolfskill: 1798-1866 Frontier Trapper to California Ranchero*. Wilson's book, published in 1965, is a compre-hensive look at his life and, until now, the only book written entirely about him. I also poured over the meticulous ledgers that William kept

Elena Wolfskill as Queen of Los Angeles
Courtesy of Elena Wolfskill Thornton

of his business transactions as well as his Old Spanish Trail ledger, a copy of which is located in the archives at the Huntington Library in San Marino, California. However, William left little written material about his personal life and thoughts with one exception—his letters to his brother, John Reid Wolfskill, that we will read in later chapters. In telling **William's Story**, I have relied on historical fact. Dialogue drawn from historical sources is footnoted. Other dialogue is my creation, extrapolated from a collection of facts to paint a portrait of a man who never looked back in his quest to explore and test the world.

The second part of every chapter is the section called **Personal Observations and Research**, which contain descriptions of my journey of discovery as my husband, Rich, and I retraced William Wolfskill's footsteps through Kentucky, Missouri, Kansas, Oklahoma, New Mexico, Utah, Nevada and California. We wanted to meet the man in his environment, which meant going to where he had lived, trapped and traveled. In this section, I also include information that helped me dig more deeply into my family roots. The thrill of connecting with other Wolfskill descendants and finding pieces of my genealogical puzzle have kept me going over the years and transformed me into a lover of genealogy and history.

In 2006, our journey of exploration began when Rich and I made plans to drive along the Santa Fe Trail to get an insight into William's journey with Captain William Becknell's second expedition to Santa Fe in 1822. Rich, a history buff, armchair archeologist and rock hound, proved to be my enthusiastic companion as we traveled to Franklin, Missouri, the departure point of the early caravans that traveled over the Santa Fe Trail. William Becknell's expedition of 21 men began their journey on May 22, 1822, from Franklin,[1] with three wagons laden with calico, muslin, hardware, buttons, knives and clothing—items Becknell knew would bring big profits in Santa Fe.

It was through Franklin's newspaper, the *Missouri Intelligencer*, that Captain William Becknell, a Missouri trader, advertised for his first expedition over the Santa Fe Trail in 1821. His notice in the newspaper stated that he was looking for "a company of men destined to the westward for the purpose of trading horses, mules, and catching wild animals of every description..."[2] On his first expedition in 1821, Becknell took pack mules and traveled over the Raton Pass in present-day New Mexico entering Santa Fe from the north. Becknell sold all of the items he had brought from Missouri and returned to Franklin a richer man. That first expedition had proved to be a financial success and opened the door to increased trade with the city of Santa Fe. Under Spanish rule, Santa Fe was closed to American traders, but after Mexico won its independence from Spain in 1821, trade restrictions were loosened and the people of Santa Fe clamored for items from the United States.

Becknell was glad to oblige by bringing more goods on his second expedition, which departed from the bustling town of Franklin with 24-year-old William Wolfskill as part of his caravan. Born in Madison County, Kentucky, on March 20, 1798,[3] William and his family were part of the westward migration and moved to Missouri in 1809 where William grew up on the edge of the frontier. Toughened by the hardships of living in the wilderness, William was more than ready for the perils of the journey. He was a fine marksman and hunter, having learned early that his Kentucky long rifle was essential to his survival. After the expedition left Franklin, it traveled westward across present-day Missouri and continued southwest into present-day Kansas where Becknell decided to take the shorter desert route to Santa Fe, now known as the Cimarron Route. Rich and I traveled to Kansas and followed parts of Becknell's route over the Journey of Death or *Jornada de Muerte*, a barren expanse of desert stretching for miles between the Arkansas and Cimarron rivers in southwestern Kansas. We learn about William's near death experience in the next chapter when the desert became a formidable enemy.

---

1 Archer Butler Hulbert, ed. *Southwest on the Turquoise Trail: The First Diaries on the Road to Santa Fe,*
(Colorado Springs: The Stewart Commission of Colorado College and the Denver Public Library, 1933), 65.
2 *Missouri Intelligencer,* June 25, 1821, page 3, column 5.
3 H.D. Barrows, "William Wolfskill, The Pioneer," *Annual Publication of the Historical Society of Southern California (1902):* 287.

CHAPTER 2

SANTA FE BOUND

William's Story

"Water, I need water," William whispered to himself as Becknell's expedition made its way across the flatlands of Kansas.

The tall, dark-haired 24-year-old adventurer considered the possibility that his life could come to an end in the middle of nowhere. The caravan, which had left the Arkansas River several days earlier, encountered nothing but dry, desolate land—and no water.[4]

The summer sun was unrelenting as the men tried to ration their water. William's throat screamed for even a drop. He tried swallowing but his saliva had all but disappeared in the heat. As sweat rolled down his face and neck, he attempted to take a sip of water, but his canteen was completely empty. Becknell ordered his men to cut the ears off their mules and drink their blood.[5]

When the wagons stopped, William's friend Ewing Young came over, his face red and sweaty. A carpenter by trade, Ewing was strong and resourceful, the kind of person you needed out on the trail.[6]

"What a hell hole," Ewing said his voice hoarse from thirst. "Billy, let's go find us a mule."

William and Ewing chose one of their oldest mules, and then slashed the animal's ears.

"It's either the mule or us," William said as he sucked on the animal's ear and swallowed its blood. The taste was so repulsive that he quickly spit the blood out, feeling thirstier than before.

The caravan kept moving as each man prayed that a stream or river would appear. William was hallucinating when he saw pools of water wafting in the distance. Then, in a miraculous moment, a buffalo appeared. Brown, with a massive, shaggy body as tall as a large man and weighing over a thousand pounds, this animal could be their salvation. William grabbed his Kentucky long rifle, poured gunpowder down the barrel and rammed a lead ball into the barrel with a wooden rod. Placing a little more gunpowder into the pan of the rifle, he cocked the hammer, aimed at the buffalo and pulled the trigger. Bam! His shot crackled in the desert silence along with the others that rang out from rifles all around him. The buffalo moved forward as bullets entered its body and then it fell to the ground.

"He's down! We got him!" William shouted.

The buffalo was surrounded by several members of the expedition who slit open the animal's belly. The smell from the animal's insides was strong so the men momentarily pulled away. But desperately thirsty, they resumed slicing into the buffalo's stomach.

"His stomach looks bloated," said one man who punctured a hole in the stomach. A cheer went up as the murky water spurted out. Everyone crowded around the downed buffalo, each man getting a small amount of the "filthy"[7] but life-saving liquid.

"The buffalo has water in him—a river or stream must be close by," William said, his voice still cracking from thirst. "We need to look for the stream." The water from the buffalo had given them some relief but it was only temporary.

The intense heat and terrible thirst made William think ruefully of his family in Boone's Lick, Missouri. Why had he been so stubborn and insisted on taking this trip? His pa had been worried when he heard that William wanted to join Becknell's second expedition to Santa Fe. The town of Franklin had been all stirred up with talk of Becknell's successful journey in 1821, amazed that he had made a profit and brought back Mexican silver and thick New Mexican wool blankets. For William, the excitement of a new frontier had overshadowed all thought of danger and risk.

Leaving the weaker caravan members behind near the fallen buffalo, William, Ewing and a few of the strongest men went scouting for water. They would all die on this wasteland if they didn't find water. But each time William thought there was a pool or stream, it turned out to be the shimmering desert. Knowing he must stay strong to survive, he urged the others to keep going. The words barely came out of his parched throat, "Water... we'll find water somewhere soon."

"Billy, if we ever get to Santa Fe, the whiskey's on me," said Ewing.

The men struggled in silence over the barren desert. William knew he needed to keep his guard up. They had already confronted a band of Osage Indians weeks earlier when they were camped on the Arkansas River.[8] He thought back on that night when 20 of their horses had been spooked by noises and fled around midnight. Eight men from the expedition dispersed in all directions and found 18 of the missing horses. However, two men encountered a group of Osage Indians who forced them to hand over their guns and horses. The two men found their way back to camp, causing a furor among Becknell's men. Another missing member of the search party also had made his way back into camp. No one had been seriously harmed, but the incident left a deep sense of unease among the expedition members.

With each passing hour in the hot sun, William was becoming weaker and his thirst unbearable. A sudden shout from one of the men in their scouting party announced he'd found a trickle of water in the dry desert. The men rushed to the water, drank the precious liquid and filled their canteens for the others waiting at camp.

William looked up at the blue skies and relentless sun. He was exhausted and yet he had never felt so lucky. He had looked death in the eye and had won this round—his time on earth was not over. William and the scouts had been saved, and now it was up to them to rescue the others. They brought water to the rest of the group, and before long the caravan was again on its way.

Becknell and his men continued west until they reached an area named Rock Creek River.[9] There they faced what seemed to be insurmountable obstacles—steep, rocky cliffs. William felt as if every muscle in his body hurt as he and the other expedition members pushed their wagons up the boulder-strewn terrain.

Several days later Becknell and his men were rewarded by a vision of the adobe church of San Miguel del Vado,[10] the first town they encountered in present-day New Mexico. San Miguel, with its collection of earth-colored adobe houses clustered around the church, was a welcome sight for the weary expedition. "*Los Americanos, la caravana*," the local people shouted as they crowded onto the main dirt road to greet the Americans.

"Men, let's show these fine people of San Miguel what a Missouri salute is like. Fire your guns," Becknell ordered.

William remembered the captain telling him that on his first journey over the Santa Fe Trail in 1821, the people of San Miguel had given him a warm welcome.[11] Now it was Becknell's turn to show appreciation for their past hospitality. He ordered his men to shoot three rounds of ammunition into the air.[12] William's old rifle joined in the explosion of gunshots as a carnival atmosphere filled the settlement. Tired but happy to reach civilization, William walked down to the Pecos River where he splashed cool water on his sunburned face and filled up several canteens.

Later that night, William lay on the hard, cold ground looking up at the high desert skies filled with millions of stars. He reflected back on his life since leaving Franklin in May. What was pushing him to confront danger? Was this restless, adventurous spirit in his blood? William remembered the stories about his Grandpa Joseph who had left Germany as a young boy. Joseph Wolfskill was the youngest of seven tall, strapping brothers who were conscripted into Frederick the Great's celebrated Potsdam Regiment because of their height and physical strength.[13] Rather than being forced into military service, Grandpa Joseph came to America[14] where his pioneer spirit took him to Pennsylvania, North Carolina, and eventually to Madison County, Kentucky.[15]

In July of 1796, William's father, also called Joseph, fell in love with his neighbor, Sarah Reed, and asked for her hand in marriage. Her father, John Reed, was an adventurer who had left Ireland as a young man and fought in the American Revolutionary War. Joseph and Sarah were married[16] and raised a family in Madison County, Kentucky. The Wolfskill family grew until Joseph and Sarah were filled with wanderlust and decided in 1809 that the new lands out West in Missouri might offer a better life.

William realized that he was following in his grandfathers' and father's footsteps by pushing into new frontiers. But it wasn't easy to leave his Missouri home. He loved its changing landscapes of thick woods and winding rivers, especially in the spring with the arrival of new growth on the trees. Life in Santa Fe would be different from Boone's Lick for sure; still that's what intrigued him. Tomorrow they would travel on towards Santa Fe where he and Ewing Young planned to start a trapping business and make money selling beaver pelts. Ewing was a good friend, someone who could be counted on during tough times. Originally from Tennessee, Ewing had also left home like William to start a new life on the frontier.

William's eyes followed a shooting star as it hurried across the Milky Way, and he pulled his blanket around him to ward off the cool night air. This journey under Captain Becknell had tested his ability to survive extreme hardships. He knew now that he could handle whatever obstacles would come. He had much to accomplish and with God's help he would blaze new trails. He was looking forward to Santa Fe and establishing himself as a trapper.

William Wolfskill
Courtesy of Elena Wolfskill Thornton

PERSONAL OBSERVATIONS AND RESEARCH

I grew up hearing my mother talk about my great-great-grandfather, William Wolfskill, a mountain man, pioneer and visionary who has always been a legendary figure in my family. "We are daughters of California," my mother would remind me instilling fierce pride in our history as early California settlers. Later I read books and articles about my ancestor, but I wanted to meet the man in his environment.

When Rich and I decided to follow in William's footsteps, we explored his early life in Boone's Lick Country[17] near the present-day town of Boonville, Missouri, where William's family had settled after making the journey from Kentucky in 1809. The Wolfskills traveled to Missouri and settled on the edge of the frontier, near the barely explored lands of the Native American and Spanish West, joining their friends the Coopers, the Kit Carson family and other families from Kentucky's Madison County. They put down roots beside the Missouri River and cleared land for their log cabin. The land was teeming with animals making it difficult to grow food, so in the early years the Wolfskills' diet consisted mostly of wild game such as deer, turkey, elk, squirrel and rabbit. Whatever small amount of corn they were able to harvest was used to bake corn bread.[18]

The relationship between the white settlers and the Native American tribes in the area was often hostile, which led the settlers to build Cooper's Fort, Fort Kincaid and Fort Hempstead to protect themselves against attacks by the Sac, Fox, Iowa and Kickapoo tribes.[19] During the War of 1812, the British enlisted the tribes against the settlers as part of the larger war between the United States and Great Britain. The Wolfskills lived in Cooper's Fort—an oblong structure made of log houses joined together around an enclosure where the animals were locked in at night. Then in his teens, William learned the lessons of the frontier and was never without his rifle.

Cooper's Fort
Drawing of Cooper's Fort in Boone's Lick, Missouri
Photo by Conchita Thornton Marusich

To learn more about the Wolfskill family, we searched for records in a small genealogy library in Fayette, Missouri. Betty Collier, a local genealogist, helped us find records of a Howard County land purchase showing that William's father, Joseph Wolfskill, bought land along the Missouri River.

Rich and I went looking for that riverside property and for Cooper's Fort, driving through farmland on dirt roads in the river bottom area until we found a small plaque with a drawing of Cooper's Fort, now just a memory. Surrounded by cornfields, we tried hard to imagine the Wolfskill family holed up in the fort built on a slight rise. It was a rigorous life with everyone on guard against attack. The Wolfskills stayed at Cooper's Fort until the end of the hostilities in 1815.[20] Rich and I attempted to reach the old Wolfskill property, but unfortunately the land has been reclaimed by the river over the years.

Next, we stopped at Boone's Lick State Historic Park where we found the remnants of a saltwater spring where salt had been produced. A path led us down to the spring area where we saw the last vestiges of the salt works and could still smell sulfur in the standing groundwater. Daniel Boone's sons, Nathan and Daniel Morgan Boone, made a successful business out of boiling the brine from the springs in 1807,[21] salt being an important frontier commodity to preserve food and enhance its flavor. It is interesting to note that William Wolfskill's grandfather, Joseph Wolfskill, had been Daniel Boone's neighbor in North Carolina.[22]

Rich and I then searched for the town of Franklin, Missouri, starting point for the early Santa Fe Trail caravans. In 1819, it was a bustling town with over 100 log cabins, four taverns, a courthouse, two billiard halls, a printing press, several brick buildings, a two-story log cabin jail and a post office.[23] The town's location on the Missouri River made it a good resting point where traders could have a haircut, buy some whiskey or purchase supplies for their long journey. Unfortunately, Franklin's role as the beginning of the Santa Fe Trail ended in 1826 when the town was almost swept away by the Missouri River[24] causing the residents to move to higher ground and relocate to New Franklin. The once booming town was abandoned and renamed Old Franklin.

Road Sign Post in Empty Field Marking Old Franklin
Photo by Conchita Thornton Marusich

Our search for Old Franklin led us down more backcountry roads and empty fields. Over the years, the Missouri River and nature had swallowed up Old Franklin, leaving no vestige of the little town. There was little evidence left that these quiet fields had once been a busy frontier town that held the distinction of being the starting point for the earliest expeditions over the great Santa Fe Trail.

Missouri River
Photo by Conchita Thornton Marusich

Looking out over the wide and powerful Missouri River as it meandered through the green hills and farmland around Boonville, Rich and I visualized young William as he set out with Becknell's caravan. Departing from the Boone's Lick area, the group of 21 men crossed the Missouri River on the Arrow Rock ferry.[25] Before the long journey, William Wolfskill would have filled his barrels with water at the Big Spring watering hole, a short walk from the ferry. Rich and I hiked to the Big Spring area and wondered how William's family felt watching their eldest son leave with Becknell's small expedition. They must have been worried not knowing if they would ever see William again.

Rich and I said goodbye to the rolling hills of Missouri and headed towards the flatter prairies of Kansas. When we drove through the town of Cimarron in western Kansas, it was hard to imagine that this land was once the beginning of the feared Journey of Death or *Jornada de Muerte*, where Becknell's second expedition almost ended in death and tragedy. Zipping along U.S. Highway 50,[26] Rich and I wondered what motivated William to leave his family and friends in Missouri and travel for months over unknown territory on the road to Santa Fe.

---

4 http://newmexicohistory.org/places/cimarron-cutoff-of-the-santa-fe-trail Albert Pike, an early traveler on the trail, described the area as being very barren and dry, with little vegetation. Accessed 12-1-16.

5 Josiah Gregg, *Commerce of the Prairies*, ed. by Max L. Moorhead (Norman: University of Oklahoma Press, 1954), 14.

6 Harvey L. Carter, "Ewing Young," in *Trappers of the Far West*, ed. Le Roy R. Hafen (Arthur H. Clark. 1965;
reprint, Lincoln and London: University of Nebraska Press/First Bison Book Edition, 1983): 51-52.

7 Gregg, *Commerce of the Prairies*, 15. At a later date Josiah Gregg heard a member of this expedition refer to the water from the buffalo's stomach as "filthy" yet describing it as an "exquisite delight" since it saved their lives.

8 Archer Butler Hulbert, ed. *Southwest on the Turquoise Trail: The First Diaries on the Road to Santa Fe*, 66.

9 Ibid., 67.

10 Ibid.

11 Ibid., 63.

12 Ibid., 67.

13 Iris Higbie Wilson, *William Wolfskill: 1798-1866 Frontier Trapper to California Ranchero* (Glendale, California: The Arthur H. Clark Company, 1965), 22. According to Wolfskill family history, young Joseph Wolfskehl fled Germany in 1742 to escape Frederick the Great's guard. Higbie Wilson wrote that this story was corroborated by Dr. William Wolfskehl in 1870 while visiting San Francisco from Germany.

14 Robert W. Ramsey, *Carolina Cradle: Settlement of the Northwest Carolina Frontier, 1747-1762* (Chapel Hill: The University of North Carolina Press, 1964), 214. A person named Joseph Wolfskehl, age 14, is mentioned on the passenger list of the ship, Loyal Judith, which arrived from Rotterdam, Germany in 1743. It is possible that passenger was William's grandfather.

15 Higbie Wilson, *William Wolfskill: 1798-1866 Frontier Trapper to California Ranchero*, 21-23.

16 "Kentucky, County Marriages, 1797-1954," database with images, FamilySearch. On July 20, 1796, John Reed, Sarah's father, gave his permission to the marriage, writing: "... Let the Bearer Joseph Wolfscale have licence to marry Sarah Reed and in so doing this shall be sufficient given under my hand..." At that time, John and Sarah spelled their last name "Reed" and Joseph's last name was "Wolfscale." Later on Reed became Reid and Wolfscale changed to Wolfskill.

17 Boone's Lick is written in two different ways: Boone's Lick and Boonslick. I have chosen to use Boone's Lick in the rest of my book. In the early days, the area was also called Boone's Lick Country.

18 http://www.rootsweb.ancestry.com/~mohoward/history.html   website   consulted 12-1-16.

19 Lyn McDaniel, ed. *Bicentennial Boonslick History* (Boonslick Historical Society: 1976), 17.

20 Higbie Wilson, *William Wolfskill: 1798-1866 Frontier Trapper to California Ranchero*, 31.

21 McDaniel, ed. *Bicentennial Boonslick History*, 10-11.

22 Higbie Wilson, *William Wolfskill: 1798-1866 Frontier Trapper to California Ranchero*, 21-22.

23 McDaniel, ed. *Bicentennial Boonslick History*, 22-23.

24 Ibid, 45.

25 Hulbert, *Southwest on the Turquoise Trail: The First Diaries on the Road to Santa Fe*, 65.

26 U.S. Highway Route 400 runs concurrently with U.S. Highway 50 in this area.

CHAPTER 3

SANTA FE TRAPPER

William's Story

Tired from the snow and cold, William and his New Mexican trapping partner made a brush hut to keep them warm. It was January 1823 and they had been trapping for beaver along the Río Grande when the weather turned. Exhausted, William lay down to rest.[27]

"*Qué mala suerte.* Bad luck to get caught in this snow," said William. "I was sure that we were going to find us some more beaver. Well, might as well get some sleep." Since arriving in Santa Fe in 1822, William had discovered that he really enjoyed the challenges of trapping for beaver, except on cold nights like this.

His partner merely grunted and started building a fire near the door of the hut. William could hear the wind howling outside, which quickly lulled him to sleep. Suddenly his deep slumber was shattered by a sharp, stunning pain that penetrated his arm and chest. William automatically reached for the rifle that was always by his side, but it was gone, and he could only find his ammunition pouch. Still groggy, William struggled to his feet and as he clutched his bleeding chest, realized that he had been shot. He called out his companion's name several times but there was no answer. He then stumbled outside in the moonlight looking for his trapping partner who had disappeared.

The snow crunched beneath his feet as he circled the hut. The cold air brought William to his senses. Was he going to die? Who had attacked them? William continued his search but there were only a few footprints. What just happened? Where was his partner? Fleetingly, William remembered his old Mexican friend who had told him to be careful of his partner, warning, "He is a bad man."[28] But William brushed those thoughts aside. His companion must have been taken captive or killed.

Bleeding from his wound, William started trudging through the snow towards the nearest settlement, Valverde, a small military outpost, which was still hours away. The cold air kept him awake. The pain in his chest reminded him that he was perhaps a thread away from death. However, his desire to live gave him the will to keep walking through the wind and snow drifts over the lonely, high desert country.

William kept telling himself to put one foot in front of the other. He thought of his family in Missouri. Guided only by the moonlight and his experience as a trapper, William walked all night and miraculously arrived at Valverde the next morning.

Despite his wounds, William was able to find the mayor or *alcalde* of the town who immediately took him to the military outpost to talk to the soldiers. William told the whole story about how he and his trapping partner had been viciously attacked. He described how a rifle ball had ripped into his chest, stopped only by a thick blanket and his right arm, which had been folded over his chest.

"My friend is missing. I hope he isn't dead," said a concerned William.

There was a knock on the door and a young soldier entered the room.

"There's a man who says that he was attacked by Indians who killed his companion, William Wolfskill," reported the young soldier.

"But I'm William Wolfskill," responded William, incredulous that his friend could be outside.

When William's trapping companion entered, he was shocked to see William.

"You survived the ambush? What a miracle," said his trapping partner, showing no sign of having been in a struggle.

Immediately sensing that William's companion was lying, the soldiers took him back to the site of the "ambush."

When they arrived at the small brush hut, the companion told how he had fought against the invaders. His voice trembled as he described how he struggled to save himself and William. He accused the Indians of shooting William and taking his gun. But the soldiers seeing only the footprints of the two trappers in the snow doubted his story and took the New Mexican back to Valverde where he was locked up.

Meanwhile, the ball was taken from William's chest since it fortunately had not penetrated into the bone. Finally, nearly frozen after several days of isolation, the companion agreed to talk.

"I'll show you where I hid the rifle, but I never tried to kill William. He's my friend. The gun went off accidentally in the hut. I had picked it up while William was asleep but I had never used a gun with a hair-trigger like that and then suddenly the rifle went off."[29]

Claiming his innocence, the companion led William, the mayor and the soldiers to the hidden gun. Glad to see his rifle again but upset with his partner, William was ready to leave Valverde. William gratefully shook the mayor's hand as he turned his back on his former partner. The soldiers then ordered the prisoner to stand up so that he could return to his cell. Realizing that all was lost, his trapping companion threw himself on his knees, opened his shirt and bared his chest, asking William to kill him if he believed him guilty. Still recuperating from his chest wound, William paused and gave him one last look of disgust. Friendship was something that William really valued, and this man had broken that trust. He didn't even feel pity for this disloyal man. Without saying a word, William turned around leaving his companion to suffer his fate with the soldiers.

William had trusted him, which made the betrayal so much worse. His old Mexican friend was right—his trapping partner was definitely a "bad man."

In February of 1824, William teamed up with his friend, Ewing Young, for a beaver trapping expedition along the San Juan River. The weather was cold when William, Ewing and a group of trappers left Taos and headed north. As the months rolled by, the various trappers split up and followed different parts of the San Juan River. William, Ewing and their friend, Isaac Slover, stayed together as a group and continued trapping.[30]

Wading close to the stream bank, William placed his last beaver trap about six inches below the water. He stepped onto the bank where he threw some mud. He carefully opened a wooden box containing some liquid and poured a little over the mud.[31] The liquid was castoreum, which came from beaver castor glands. Following an old trapper recipe that he hoped would attract the little critters, William had already added a little nutmeg, cloves and cinnamon[32] to the strong-smelling beaver oil. He splashed some water on his footsteps near the mud so that the beaver would not be scared off by his scent. William then walked back to camp where Ewing and Isaac were busy cooking deer meat for dinner. The burning wood and roasting deer sent up a pungent smell.

"I'd like a little piece of that leg. I'm hungrier than a bear," said William as he warmed his hands by the fire.

"We caught three beavers in our traps today, all with nice thick coats," said Ewing as he turned the deer meat, which was skewered on a thick branch over the fire.

"This deer meat is pretty tasty. You know, you're both good cooks." William carved another piece of meat off the deer leg.

"I think we'll be able to trap only a few more weeks," said Isaac.

"Well, I just set a new trap so let's see what I get." William was hoping to catch a few more beaver.

"The trappin's been good. I'm in no hurry to get back," responded Ewing.

The three men hungrily ate their meal and finished it off with a good dose of Taos Lightning, a spicy whiskey popular with trappers. As William fell asleep that night warmed by the flames of the fire and strong brew, he thought how lucky he was. He had adventure, good friends and a belly full of delicious food. At the end of the journey in June, William, Ewing and Isaac returned to Santa Fe bringing back over $10,000 worth of pelts.[33]

Later that year, William joined Captain Owens, his father's neighbor from Boone's Lick, Missouri, on an expedition to Chihuahua, Mexico, where horses and mules could be cheaply bought. They were successful in purchasing a herd of animals and in the fall were headed back towards Missouri.[34] William felt uneasy as he drove a herd of horses and mules through the unforgiving, northern Chihuahua Mexican desert. Extended before him were endless miles of parched horizon. Their first stop would be in Presidio del Norte, a small town on the present-day Texas-Mexico border.

"Captain Owens, this is a treacherous area. I've heard that the local Indians don't take kindly to strangers comin' through their land," said William as he rode alongside the captain.

"Billy, I've heard those stories, but I can make a lot of money on these animals if I can get them to Louisiana, and that's where we're headed." His face creased with worry, Owens seemed to age in front of William's eyes. "We need the money."

"I understand, Captain. We'll get these animals to Louisiana if we have to go through fire."

"That's Billy Wolfskill for you," said Owens. "Your pa always said you get things done." He paused for a bit. "I know I can depend on you."

The Captain's expedition continued pushing through the desert day after day. They were very close to Presidio del Norte, when a group of local Indians attacked, causing the horses and mules to stampede. The air shook as the hooves of fleeing animals pounded the earth. Left without his horse, William made his way through the dust only to find that Captain Owens and other members of the expedition had been killed in the attack. William and another survivor named Belcher came to the assistance of a companion who had been wounded and then they turned their attention to tending to the dead.

As William laid Captain Owens' body into a makeshift grave, he made a promise to his father's neighbor that he would get the animals to Louisiana if he could ever find them. It was with a heavy heart that he covered the Captain with dirt and laid him to rest in the Mexican desert far from home in Boone's Lick.

Stranded, without a way to return to Missouri, William was overjoyed when several horses and mules wandered back into their camp and still more returned over the next few days. William and Belcher were able to buy a number of animals with money they had found in Owens' belongings. As soon as possible, William and Belcher started eastward, driving the much smaller herd into present-day Texas. William's hope was to sell the animals and give the money to Owens' family. But exhaustion and the pain of his old chest wound finally wore William down. He decided to leave the horses and mules with Belcher with the promise that they would meet in Natchitoches, Louisiana, by July 4, 1825. William took a steamer up the Mississippi River to St. Louis, Missouri.[35]

He arrived in Boone's Lick, Missouri, in June of 1825. Resting up in his father's house for barely a month, William started feeling restless. It was hard to see Captain Owens' widow every Sunday at church and not feel burdened by the promise he had made to his dead friend.

"Pa, I have to go down to Louisiana and pick up the Captain's herd. I just hope that I can find Belcher and the animals. If I find 'em, I'll be gone for a few months while I drive the horses and mules up to Alabama where I can sell 'em and give the money to his wife."

"Billy, you're a good friend. I told the captain not to go to Chihuahua but he was so certain that he'd bring back some good money. His widow will sure appreciate it. It's dangerous territory so be careful."

"The weather's fine right now and I can get to Alabama before the cold sets in. Don't worry about me, Pa."

William then headed to Natchitoches, Louisiana, but not finding Belcher or the animals, he traveled west to San Felipe, in present-day Texas, located on the Brazos River, where he found his fellow mate from the Owens expedition.[36] Belcher, however, had no intention of meeting William and giving up the herd. William finally convinced him that the horses and mules needed to be sold to help the Captain's widow. After rounding up the animals, William started the long journey east to Alabama in hot and humid weather that left him drenched in sweat most days. It was particularly hard at dusk when the mosquitoes were unrelenting. At last, he reached Greensborough, Alabama, a small but growing town of log cabins.[37] William was able to sell the Captain's animals and after staying the winter, in March of 1826, he headed back to Boone's Lick, Missouri, where he handed the money over to Captain Owens' widow. He finally felt at peace.

During a visit to Franklin, a few miles from his father's home, William ran into his good friend, Ewing Young, who persuaded him to return to Santa Fe. William was ready for adventure again.

His father, Joseph Wolfskill, and William's brother, John Reid Wolfskill, were cleaning their rifles when William arrived with news of his planned departure.

"Pa, my friend, Ewing, is travelin' through the area. I saw him over in Franklin today and he asked me to join him on a trappin' expedition. But don't worry, you know that I'll be back," he said to reassure his father.

"Maybe, but I'm always thinkin' you won't return. You've got beaver trappin' fever," responded Joseph. Turning to John Reid, his young 22-year-old son, he said, "I hope you'll always stay here in Missouri. The farmin's good and it's gettin' time that you started a family."

John Reid hesitated and then answered, "Pa, you know you can always count on me when you need help. But I can't promise that I will always be livin' here. I want to see other places too."

William understood his younger brother's frustration. "You and Pa can come to Santa Fe. And I can show you where the trappin's good. What do you say, Pa?"

"I'm too old but I can see that both of you have adventure in your blood. I was like you when I was young and we came out from Kentucky. It was a long way but we made it out here. Yes, I sure remember those days..." Joseph Wolfskill's voice trailed off as he drifted into those distant memories. William was sad to leave his family in Boone's Lick but felt pulled by his trapping business back in Santa Fe and Taos.

After William and Ewing returned to Santa Fe in 1826, Ewing applied for and received "passports" from New Mexico Governor Antonio Narbona, which would allow him to trade in Sonora, Mexico.[38] However, when Ewing fell ill and was unable to travel, he asked William to head an expedition including Mountain Man Milton Sublette[39] to the Gila River. Several additional trappers led by Maurice Le Duc and Thomas Smith, later known as Peg-Leg Smith, became part of William's expedition.[40] After a number of weeks trapping on the Gila, William's party encountered a group of Apaches who at first seemed friendly and even invited the trappers to share their food. However, toward the end of the meal, an Apache shot an arrow at one of William's animals, which signaled impending trouble. Hoping to prevent any violence, William and his party quickly left. However, when Thomas Smith and Milton Sublette tried to save their beaver traps, they were chased away by a volley of arrows from the Apaches. The only injury was to Milton, who took an arrow in the leg and was carried to safety by Thomas Smith.[41] Dejected over the loss of their beaver traps but undaunted by the attack, William and the group returned to Santa Fe already planning their next expedition when they could again test their survival skills and physical endurance.

~⁓

Personal Observations and Research

Beaver pelts turned out to be very important in William Wolfskill's life. When he first arrived in Santa Fe from Missouri in the summer of 1822, William was quickly swept up into the life of a trapper. At that time, beaver fur was fashionable in Europe and the eastern cities of the United States. People were insatiable in their desire to wear beaver fur. Women added it to their favorite bonnets, wore beaver as shawls and used the fur as trim for their silk dresses. A well-dressed man had to be seen in a top hat made from beaver fur.

Trapping beaver turned into William's main occupation once he settled down in Santa Fe. William and Ewing Young became business partners, eventually co-owning a store in Taos,[42] and running trapping expeditions out of Santa Fe and Taos. They associated with trappers who became famous mountain men, like Peg-Leg Smith and Milton Sublette as mentioned in the last story.

These mountain men were daring, larger-than-life individuals who embraced the challenges of trapping for beaver under very tough conditions. Often living outdoors for months at a time and enduring extreme temperature changes, insect invasions and ferocious animals, the mountain men enjoyed the thrill of finding beaver with their thick coats. Milton Sublette, a mountain man originally from Kentucky and one of eight children, was a large man who stood more than six feet tall and was described as being "reckless of life and money."[43] Thomas Smith, later known as Peg-Leg Smith, had a wooden leg he used after an Indian shot out his knee. Isaac Slover, a farmer from Pennsylvania, was in his late forties when he joined William and Ewing in 1824 on their successful trapping expedition on the San Juan River. Toughened by his time as a farmer and mountain man, Isaac Slover lived a long life and hunted grizzlies into his seventies.[44]

When I first started reading about William Wolfskill trapping for beaver pelts, I must admit that it was hard to learn these animals were killed in such large numbers that they almost became extinct in the American West by the mid-1800s due to over trapping. Luckily for the beaver population, fur eventually went out of fashion. Personally, I find the beaver to be a very interesting animal with its bright eyes and beautiful fur. One of my favorite stories comes from my time working as a researcher for the television show, "Real People." We filmed an episode about the Beaver Lady, Dorothy Richards, and her 1200 acre beaver sanctuary in upstate New York. Rich and I stayed at her home called Beaversprite where we met Nicky, her pet beaver, who lived in a pool that Dorothy built in her basement. A dedicated animal lover, Dorothy worked her entire life to help preserve the beaver population and after her death, her home became a nature center.

The harrowing story of William's brush with death in Valverde was recounted by Henry Dwight (H.D.) Barrows in his article called "William Wolfskill, The Pioneer." Barrows only refers to William's trapping partner as the "New Mexican" companion who, therefore, remains anonymous in this story. At that time, present-day New Mexico was part of Mexico, which had won its independence from Spain in 1821. Since all the people in this story were from New Mexico, with the exception of William, they obviously would have been speaking in Spanish. Having arrived in Santa Fe in the summer of 1822, William could have learned enough Spanish in approximately 6 months to communicate well in the language, especially given that he was trapping with a "New Mexican."

After reading Barrow's account, Rich and I traveled to the area south of present-day Socorro, New Mexico, and tried to find Valverde, which unfortunately no longer exists. The area is barren, high desert located along the Río Grande. Valverde has an interesting history. Josiah Gregg, who wrote about his travels on the Santa Fe Trail in his book, *Commerce of the Prairies*, noted that by 1839 Valverde had fallen into ruins after attacks by Native Americans forced its residents to abandon the town.[45] Twenty-three years later, on February 20-21, 1862, Valverde became the site of a bloody battle in the Civil War between the Confederate and Union solders along the banks of the Río Grande. The Confederates won the battle but suffered a heavy loss of life. Four months later, the Confederates were forced to leave the New Mexico Territory.[46]

---

27 H.D. Barrows, "William Wolfskill, The Pioneer," 287.

28 Ibid., 289.

29 Ibid., 288.

30 Carter, "Ewing Young," in *Trappers of the Far West*, 52. David Weber, *The Taos Trappers: The Fur Trade in the Far Southwest 1540-1846* (Norman: University of Oklahoma Press, 1971), 67.

31 Osborne Russell, *Journal of a Trapper*, ed. Aubrey L. Haines (Oregon Historical Society: 1955; Reprint, Lincoln/London: University of Nebraska Press/First Bison Book Edition, 1965), 150. These details are from Osborne Russell's description of setting a beaver trap.

32 *The Journals of Lewis and Clark*, ed. Bernard De Voto (Boston: The American Heritage Library, Houghton Mifflin Company,1953), 303. This gives the recipe of preparing beaver bait which has been used by trappers throughout the years.

33 Carter, "Ewing Young," in *Trappers of the Far West*, 52.

34 H.D. Barrows, The Story of an Old Pioneer," *Wilmington Journal, October 20, 1866.*

35 Ibid.

36 Ibid.

37 William Edward Wadsworth Yerby, *The History of Greensboro, Alabama, From its Earliest Settlement*, (Montgomery, Alabama: Paragon Press, 1908), 9.

38 Higbie Wilson, *William Wolfskill: 1798-1866 Frontier Trapper to California Ranchero*, 49-50.

39 Barrows, "William Wolfskill, the Pioneer," 290. Higbie Wilson, *William Wolfskill: 1798-1866 Frontier Trapper to California Ranchero*, 50, 53. Barrows, "The Story of an Old Pioneer," *Wilmington Journal, October 20, 1866.*

40 "The Story of An Old Trapper," *The San Francisco Bulletin Company*, October 26, 1866. In Peg-Leg Smith's obituary, it was claimed that this event occurred when Peg-Leg led a group of trappers including Milton Sublette to the Gila River. However, I am following H.D. Barrows' version that had William Wolfskill as the leader of this expedition, which included Peg-Leg Smith and Milton Sublette. I have also incorporated some of the details from Peg-Leg Smith's obituary since the stories told by Barrows' and Peg-Leg Smith appear to be the same story.

41 "The Story of an Old Trapper." Higbie Wilson, *William Wolfskill: 1798-1866 Frontier Trapper to California Ranchero*, 53.

42 Carter, "Ewing Young," in *Trappers of the Far West*, 57.

43 Doyce Nunis, "Milton G Sublette," in *Trappers of the Far West*," ed. by Le Roy R. Hafen (Arthur H. Clark. 1965; reprint, Lincoln and London: University of Nebraska Press/First Bison Book Edition, 1983), 106.

44 Old Spanish Trail Association, http://oldspanishtrail.org/assets/downloads/trailpersonalityprofile-slover.pdf Accessed 12-1-16.

45 Gregg, *Commerce of the Prairies*, ed. by Max L. Moorhead, 269.

46 https://www.nps.gov/abpp/battles/nm001.htm

CHAPTER 4

Traveling the Santa Fe Trail

William's Story

In the fall of 1827, William, his trading partner, Thomas Talbot, and five other traders headed east toward Missouri on the Santa Fe Trail herding approximately 170 horses and mules they had purchased in northern Mexico.[47] On October 12, 1827, as customary every night on the trail, they set up camp and placed several men near the horses and mules to guard them against thieves. William pulled his buffalo skin blanket around him to ward off the cold October evening air. He thought back on the previous year that he and the other traders had spent in northern Mexico selling goods from Missouri so that they could purchase a large group of horses and mules. It had been a hard trip and at last they would make back their money by selling their animals in Missouri. Kit Carson's brothers, William and Robert, had joined William on this trip.[48] The Wolfskill and Carson families were long-time friends from the time they had all been neighbors in Madison County, Kentucky, and continued the friendship after their resettlement in Missouri.

William and his group had endured many hardships over their time in Mexico and now they were almost home. William savored the moment and was just about to nod off when the sound of gunshots rang out through the camp and a group of about 30 Pawnee

Indians, guns in hand, advanced toward the animals until they were about 25 yards away.

Reaching for his rifle, William heard blood-curdling "war whoops," gunshots and the shaking of rattles. The mules and horses, terrified by the strange noises, stampeded from the camp. The Pawnees chased the fleeing animals and whipped them with their bowstrings to make them go even faster.

"Men, follow those bandits," shouted William as he mounted one of the remaining horses, which turned out to be older and slow-moving. His adrenaline pumping, William tried to spur on his horse but the animal could not keep up with the fast-moving runaways. Soon the animals and the Pawnees had disappeared.

William returned to camp a cold, upset and dejected man. A year's worth of work in Mexico was gone in an instant. Thomas, his partner, sat down on the log next to William as frustration poured out of him.

"Why isn't the gov'ment doin' more to protect us? I thought they'd made treaties with the diffr'ent tribes. We should demand that they pay us for our losses. When we get to Boone's Lick, we're goin' to write a letter to the United States gov'ment and ask 'em to help us."

William nodded his head in agreement. All that work and out of their entire herd only three animals remained.

"They got all the good animals and left us with the 'gentle'[49] ones that can hardly move," William said as he stoked the fire. "We must ask for justice. We've lost everythin'."

That night William could not sleep, thinking about his lost horses and mules. The next day William and the group resumed their search for the runaway herd without success until a miracle happened. Back at camp, they were surprised to see that 66 horses and mules had wandered back on their own. Somewhat placated by the return of approximately one third of their animals, William, Thomas and the group continued on to Missouri arriving in November 1827. Still upset that they had lost more than 100 animals on the Santa Fe Trail, William, Thomas and five other members of their group wrote a letter to the United States Congress asking for reimbursement for their stolen horses and mules.

"To the honorable… Senate and House of Representatives of the United States in Congress assembled…" After a long narration of how they had been robbed of more than 100 horses and mules on the Santa Fe Trail, which they believed was under the protection of the government, they ended the letter stating:

"Wherefore your Petitioners…humbly pray relief … by being allowed such sums as may be found just, to be paid them respectively by authority of a law making an appropriation in their behalf."[50]

The traders knew that their petition was a long shot since there was no law requiring the government to help pay for their loss. When the request was denied,[51] William and his men were disappointed but felt consoled that they at least had tried to get reimbursement for their stolen animals.

The winter months passed uneventfully as William helped his family in Missouri, traveling once to Kentucky on business for his father. But again, his restlessness started gnawing away as the spring of 1828 approached and William planned for his next journey. He bought a wagon and oxen in order to haul needed goods over the trail and make some money selling them in Santa Fe and Taos.[52] Since William had made his first trip with Captain William Becknell in 1822, the Santa Fe Trail had increased in popularity, bringing many traders to New Mexico.

As he finished packing his wagon, William knew his departure would again cause pain for his father.

"I'll be travelin' back here soon enough. You just can't get rid of me," said William with a laugh to his father and brother who had brought out some food for the journey.

"Son, I know you have to go to Santa Fe. There is nothin' in Missouri to hold you here. But promise me that no matter what happens, you'll always take care of your brothers and sisters," said Joseph Wolfskill.

"Billy, if you don't return home soon then I'll come and visit you wherever you are," said John Reid. "Good luck, and write us often if you can."

"Like I said to you many times, there's lots of beaver trappin' and good money to be made if you come to Santa Fe." William said as he slapped his brother on the back.

"Billy, don't you be fillin' your brother with wild ideas of leavin' home," said their father. "He's doin' just fine right where he is."

William had felt close to his younger brother since they were boys at Cooper's Fort in Missouri. He thought back on how John Reid had been the shoemaker for the family[53], which often caused him to miss out when the other boys went fox or possum hunting. He recalled how his younger brother hated being holed up inside the fort during the raids in the War of 1812. William hoped that John Reid would visit him in Santa Fe so that they could go trapping together.

"Little brother, you're always welcome. I could sure use your help with my business. Just keep an eye on our pa."

William gave his father a last hug as he said his goodbyes.

"Follow your dreams, Billy," encouraged his father. "Here, take this bread with you on your journey." Standing by his wagon, William signaled to the oxen it was time to leave.

"Move on out, we're headin' back to Santa Fe," William said. As the wagon lurched forward, William took a last look at his family and waved goodbye feeling a pang of sadness but also excitement about the trip ahead of him. "I'll see you before the winter," he shouted as he walked alongside his wagon, but his destiny lay elsewhere. He would never return to Boone's Lick.[54]

William made his last journey over the Santa Fe Trail that spring of 1828 joining a large caravan of wagons. The woods of Missouri soon gave way to the tall grasses of present-day eastern Kansas.[55] The prairie seemed to stretch out forever and touch the blue skies as the caravan made its way day after day of grass, mud and, sometimes, rain. So much had happened since he had traveled across this land with William Becknell only six years earlier. Then, they were trailblazers and danger seemed to lurk behind every rock. Now, with more traders making their way westward, the route was marked with wagon wheel ruts that deepened with each passing month. As the caravan made its way along the approximately 900-mile-trail, William looked forward to returning to Santa Fe and his friends again. After a long day on the Trail, Wolfskill dreamed about trapping beaver in the cool streams of New Mexico. Finally, the caravan started climbing into the high desert. Soon William arrived in Santa Fe after a long but uneventful trip, one so different from his first expedition six years earlier when he almost died on the Journey of Death in Kansas.

~‿ꝰ

PERSONAL OBSERVATIONS AND RESEARCH

After his historic journey with William Becknell's second expedition in 1822, William Wolfskill made several more trips on the Santa Fe Trail to visit his family in Missouri and transport goods and animals for sale. William's final journey occurred in 1827 when he and six other traders drove a large herd of horses and mules from Santa Fe to Boone's Lick, Missouri. They felt more secure on the trail since the United States government had authorized a bill in 1825 to survey the road between the Missouri frontier and New Mexico as well as negotiate the right of travelers to pass through the Indian lands.[56] Under Santa Fe road commissioners, George Sibley, Benjamin Reeves and Thomas Mather, the road to Santa Fe was surveyed. They also negotiated treaties with the Kansa and Osage tribes that gave free use of the road to the United States in return for monetary compensation.[57]

On October 12, 1827, William and his caravan stopped for the night about 25 miles west of Pawnee Fork Crossing at the Arkansas River[58] close to present-day Larned, Kansas. At that time, it was a lonely stretch of plains far from any settlements. Fort Larned, which provided important protection to travelers on the Santa Fe Trail didn't come into existence until 1860,[59] while the city of Larned dates from 1873. The lack of towns and settlements meant that early traders were on their own in these remote areas.

To find out more about William's journey near Larned, Kansas, Rich and I visited local historian, David Clapsaddle, an expert on the Santa Fe Trail from Pawnee Rock to Dodge City, Kansas, and author of a book about the wet and dry routes of the Trail through that area. David and his wife, Alice, met us at the southwest edge of Larned, where David and his local chapter of the Santa Fe Trail Association built the Zebulon Pike Memorial Plaza to commemorate explorer Zebulon Pike's journey through the area in 1806. William Becknell used a number of Pike's maps and notes during his inaugural trip on the Santa Fe Trail in 1821.[60] The plaza is close to where the Pawnee Fork Crossing intersected with the Arkansas River during William Wolfskill's time. David recounted how the Pawnee River would often flood, forcing the Santa Fe travelers to wait days even weeks before they could ford the river.

David informed us that Kansas historian, Louise Barry, wrote that William Wolfskill and his fellow traders were eventually reimbursed for the horses and mules stolen by the Pawnees. According to Barry, William received $105 on October 15, 1849, under an act of Congress approved on March 3, 1849. Barry also stated that William and his group had most likely camped close to Little Coon Creek, located near the present-day town of Kinsley, Kansas, about 25 miles from Larned.[61] Rich and I drove west on U.S. Highway 56 to the outskirts of Kinsley, which wasn't built until 1872.[62] As we looked out over Coon Creek, we imagined William and his group settling in on October 12, 1827, perhaps with the wind blowing hard as it often does on the plains.

47 James W. Covington, ed., "A Robbery on the Santa Fe Trail 1827," ed., *Kansas Historical Quarterly*, Vol. XXI, No.7 (Autumn 1955): 560-63. http://www.kshs.org/p/a-robbery-on-the-santa-fe-trail-1827/13109 Accessed 12-1-16. The other traders included Thomas Talbot, Elisha Stanley, James Collins, Edwin M. Ryland, James Fielding and Solomon Houck.
48 Higbie Wilson, *William Wolfskill: 1798-1866 Frontier Trapper to California Ranchero*, 55.
49 Covington, ed., "A Robbery on the Santa Fe Trail 1827," 560-563.
50 Ibid.
51 Ibid.
52 Barrows, "The Story of an Old Pioneer," *Wilmington Journal*.
53 Edward Wolfskill also known as Ned, *A Few of the Things I Remember as Told Me by My Father, the Late J.R. Wolfskill*, unpublished manuscript in Special Collections/General Library, UC Davis: 1925, 2.
54 The traders traveling over the Santa Fe Trail many times walked alongside their wagons in order to reduce the weight of the wagons thereby making it an easier load for the oxen to pull.
55 Barrows, "The Story of an Old Pioneer," *Wilmington Journal*.
56 James W. Covington, ed., "A Robbery on the Santa Fe Trail."
57 Louise Barry, *The Beginning of the West: Annals of the Kansas Gateway to the American West 1540-1854*,
(Topeka, Kansas: Kansas State Historical Society, 1972), 118-123.

58 Covington, ed., "A Robbery on the Santa Fe Trail 1827," 560-563.

59 Buchanan and McCauley, *Roadside Kansas*, (Lawrence, Kansas: University Press of Kansas, 1987, 2010), 295. Camp Alert, a temporary military structure, was built in 1859, while Fort Larned, a permanent post, was built in 1860.

60 http://www.santafetrailresearch.com/pike/plaza.html Accessed 12-1-16. http://santafetrailresearch.com/directory/of-sft-sites.html This auto tour guide and Santa Fe Trail Directory complied by David Clapsaddle and his chapter shows the Trail sites in the Wet/Dry Routes part of the Santa Fe Trail. Accessed 1-30-17.

61 Barry, *The Beginning of the West: Annals of the Kansas Gateway to the American West 1540-1854*, 146.

62 Buchanan and McCauley, *Roadside Kansas*, 294.

CHAPTER 5

BLAZING THE OLD SPANISH TRAIL

William's Story

William Wolfskill gave the signal to his band of trappers to start moving out, all of them filled with the excitement of beginning a new journey that would take them across unknown lands to California. As they drove their oxen, mules and horses through the small settlement of Abiquiu, New Mexico,[63] with its cluster of earth-colored adobe houses and dirt alleyways, William knew this would be the last town they would see for months. He had waited out the summer heat until late September of 1830, and now was anxious to be on his way before the harsh winter months set in. William also was eager to meet up with Ewing Young who had gone to trap beaver in California.

Traveling under a bright blue sky filled with billowing white clouds, William and his men entered into a magnificent if desolate landscape of red cliffs and multicolored rock formations. Piñon pines, cholla cactus and sagebrush dotted the red earth. In the distance loomed a large mountain looking as though its summit had been cut off by God to form a tabletop. Dressed in an antelope skin shirt, breeches, leggings, a buckskin coat, moccasins,[64] and a black felt hat that partly covered his shoulder-length dark hair, William was ready for many months of travel. His pistol and butcher knife were attached to his leather belt. He carried his rifle with a powder horn and ammunition pouch hung across his chest.

In preparation for this trip, William had bought four oxen[65] to eat along the trail when food became scarce. He had also stocked up on important items such as tobacco and gunpowder, which he would sell later on the trail for $1.50 a pound, as well as gun flints that would bring three cents each.[66] Combs, soap, knives, blankets, guns, rifles and flour would also sell well, but William did not bring any Taos Lightning. He knew drinking too much liquor could cause fights or worse between his men when things became tough on the trail.[67]

His group was a motley collection made up of mountain men who thrived on the challenges of the wilderness. His fellow trapper and friend, George Yount, had already traveled through parts of the route they were about to follow. Blond, with a strong chin, a prominent nose and penetrating blue eyes,[68] George would be an enormous help on the trip. William had known George since they were both in their teen years surviving on the Missouri frontier. During the War of 1812, George, who was four years older than William, had fought as a young soldier and protected the various forts near the Boone's Lick area, including Cooper's Fort, where the Wolfskill family lived. It gave William comfort that George had defended the settlers back in Missouri and would come through again if needed.

George came alongside William.

"Billy, the weather looks mighty good."

"Sure does. I'm glad you're with us, George. Good to have you along."

"Well me and my men are ready for anythin' that happens," said George.

"I know and I'm countin' on you to keep a watch on things especially when we hit the Mojave. I'm sure glad that Ziba Branch has joined us, too. He's a good man," said William.

Like William, Ziba had traveled on the Santa Fe Trail from Missouri and experienced the hardships of traveling though rough terrain. Originally from New York, Ziba was a strong and resourceful trapper who understood how to survive in the wilderness.

William and George knew they would be crossing through dangerous territory and needed men who were trustworthy and self-reliant. As the group headed north, William could not know that he would never again return to Santa Fe, Abiquiu, Taos or New Mexico.

The expedition followed the Dolores River and headed northwest into present-day Utah until they reached the Colorado River "just below the head of the Dolores River."[69] It was a humbling sight for the travelers as they made their way through the stark canyons of Utah. The weather turned cold as they continued north, passing near the Green River. Fearful of attacks, William kept a close watch on the horizon for intruders.

They still had not seen many Indians when they encountered a funeral ceremony for a Ute chief.[70] Even though the tribe was in deep mourning, its leaders invited William's group to join the funeral.

Several of the Utes recognized George Yount from his previous travels in this area and addressed him as the chief of the expedition.[71] George protested that William was the leader of the group since most of the trappers were his men, but after much discussion among themselves, the Utes shook their heads and would only acknowledge George as the leader.[72] William felt uneasy and had several of his men positioned nearby to be watchful of any sudden changes in the mood of the crowd. So far, the Utes had been friendly, but William did not want to upset them in any way.

"George, they believe you're the chief. So, I'll be your humble helper." William said with a smile and made a slight bow to his friend.

"Now let's give 'em the presents they're hopin' for," said William, at which point George ordered that knives, tobacco, beads and other trinkets be spread on the ground in front of the Utes. Then George rose and spoke in exaggerated images about the president of the United States.

"[I speak to you] of the great and mighty Pale Father at Washington and of his mighty Rifles - of his Big Cabins and his many Braves... Whose Big Gun makes the Thunder."[73]

William was amused with his friend's efforts at grandiose imagery.

The Utes listened to the description of the Great Father in Washington but were mainly interested in receiving their gifts of knives, tobacco, beads and awls.

After this presentation, the mourning continued as the dead chief's belongings were piled on his body and burned.[74] The chief was now on his way to the next life bringing with him all of his possessions. William watched the flames yet still kept a close eye on the mourners. Would they turn once the burning was done? He looked in Ziba Branch's direction. Their glances locked for a moment, and Ziba nodded as a signal that he, too, was keeping a close watch.

An elder started singing in the Ute language while others joined the chanting.

"They are singing about the chief and how brave he was," said one of the Utes to William.[75]

The fire slowly died out and turned to red-hot embers. William and his men stood for a long time listening to the chanting, mesmerized by its rhythms. After the funeral, the Utes, impressed with the trappers' respect during the ceremony, promised that they would be protected from "harm"[76] while on Ute lands.

When William and his men resumed their journey, they arrived in an area that was barren and remote.[77] The expedition made its way through mounds of grey rocks, endless stretches of sagebrush-covered desert, punctuated here and there with an occasional tree, sudden rock formations of sandstone, and hills of thick, hard clay-like earth. Water was almost non-existent except for a random stream, usually a trickle that would appear and then disappear back into the unforgiving desert. Dust was everywhere. William's eyes itched and his skin had turned brown from the dust.

They pushed on until they arrived at a spot Yount later called Pleasant Valley,[78] which turned out to be as lovely as its name.

"This is just like heaven," said William as he sat down on a fallen log. All around were forests, streams and green pastures. After the hard travel of the past few days, this was a moment to savor. George, who had been cleaning his rifle, stopped to look at the sun disappearing behind the mountains.

The two men sat pensively for a few minutes. William broke the silence.

"I wish we could stay here for at least another day but I'm worried about the weather."

"Could snow soon. The weather can change real fast," said George.

"That happened last year when I was trappin' for beaver," said William. "We'll have to get movin' tomorrow."

"What are you goin' to do when we get to California?" George asked, curious about William's plans.

"Probably hunt for beaver if I can ever find Ewing Young. Then turn around and head back to Santa Fe. What about you?"

"I've heard California's got land that's good for growin' and raisin' some cattle. Maybe I'll stay. We'll see," said George as he finished cleaning his rifle.

"Good for growin'," repeated William. "I like the sound of that."

After they left Pleasant Valley, snow blanketed the landscape covering the juniper bushes and trees. One night as William and his men were setting up camp, they encountered a lone member of the Paiute tribe, who was terrified at being discovered by them. The Paiute tried to run but was hampered by the snowdrifts. He led William's group to others in his tribe, who were equally afraid of the white men. After communicating through sign language, William calmed the frightened Paiutes by offering them gifts of beads, awls, and knives, which seemed to distract them.[79] William and his men then returned to their camp and settled in for a long, wintery night.

As the expedition pushed on, they reached Clear Creek where William and George took the wrong turn. Instead of following the known trail established by mountain man, Jedediah Smith, Wolfskill's expedition turned south.[80] They were engulfed in a brutal winter storm as they crossed a high plateau near present-day Panguitch, Utah.

"Men, stay close to the animals. They're warmer than we are," said William. "We've got to start makin' a shelter now."

Knowing they could perish in the storm, they dug deeply into the snow in an effort to stay warm. They rounded up the animals and took out all their thick blankets and beaver skins, which they laid over the snow like a carpet.[81] As the winds howled around them and the snowdrifts piled higher and higher, William and his group tried to remain calm.

The men cut tree branches and started a fire that they kept going night and day in hopes of generating at least a little warmth. Running water came from the nearby stream the trappers kept accessible by constantly breaking through the ice. Days and nights crawled by and merged into an eternity while the snow grew thicker and the wind blew fiercely. The men huddled with the animals to keep warm. Tempers flared as they grew tired of their captivity, but the trappers knew that their survival depended on staying strong as a group. Gradually the snowfall lessened and rain took its place, leaving a thick layer of ice that froze over everything.

Once the snow and rain stopped, William and George climbed up the mountain until they reached a lookout. Stretched before them, lay a never-ending landscape of snow-capped mountains, which seemed to blend with the sky. Their hopes of finding a way out vanished because all landmarks were hidden beneath the thick blanket of interminable snowdrifts.[82]

When the weather cleared up, William's group started down the mountain, cold and demoralized. Each man wondered whether they would find their way to California. Several days of marching through the wet snow further dampened their spirits.

"We're running low on food," said William. "We have only one more ox we can kill. After that we're down to the horses and mules." He shuddered as he thought back on his time on the Santa Fe Trail when, desperate for water, Captain Becknell had ordered them to suck blood from a mule's ear they had cut off.

"Let's face it. The men are tired and impatient," said George, reporting the daily rumblings of the men. "They want to get to California." After the endless snow, William and George were as frustrated as their men.

"I know they're tired. But now more than ever, they need to keep their spirits up. This is the most dangerous time for us—when we're tired and hungry," replied William. "I've seen reasonable men do terrible things when they become desperate."

"We have to make sure that no fightin' breaks out," George said, worried that the men could turn against each other. "The men are on edge."

When the expedition finally straggled out of the mountains, they killed their last ox.[83] As the days dragged on, they started their descent to the Virgin River, which took them to the Colorado River.

By the time the expedition arrived at the Mojave Indian villages, William's men were exhausted, hungry and suspicious. There had been deadly conflict between the Mojave Tribe and previous groups of trappers, so William ordered his men to mount a swivel gun on a mule to be ready at all times in case they were attacked.[84] Instead, William's group was given a warm welcome by the Mojave Indians, who gave them corn bread, dried pumpkins and small white beans in exchange for the red cloth and knives offered by the trappers.[85] Though they had anticipated trouble, Wolfskill's men were treated well and continued on their journey.

Once they left the Mojave villages, William's expedition followed the Mojave Indian trails over long stretches of desert toward the San Bernardino Mountains. Plagued by the lack of provisions, they traveled as quickly as they could and on February 5, 1831, arrived at Antonio María Lugo's ranch.[86] After leaving their men at the ranch to rest up, William and George mounted their tired horses and headed out to look for the San Gabriel Mission. They pressed their horses without a break until they came to a place where suddenly hundreds, perhaps thousands of cattle stretched out before them. The two men stopped in amazement.

"I've never seen so many cattle together in one place!" said George. "This is unbelievable! And look how green these hills are."

"The soil looks good," replied William as he gazed out over the cattle grazing on wild oats. "This just might be a great place for farmin'."

William thought of his days as a young boy in Missouri when he helped his ma and pa raise vegetables. He loved working the land and often thought about settling down. Perhaps this new territory might be the place to start his own family.

Making their way through the herd, William and George were even more surprised to learn from a local *vaquero* or cowboy that all this land and all these animals belonged to the San Gabriel Mission.[87]

"Do you think the good father will run us off if we ask for help?" said William as he stroked his scraggly beard. "We sure don't look very respectable."

"We have no choice but to throw ourselves at his mercy," responded George with a laugh. After months on the trail, the trappers were in need of a bath, a good shave and some clean clothes.

Father José Bernardo Sánchez, head of the San Gabriel Mission, always enjoyed hearing news and invited the weary travelers to stay at the mission.

After several days of hospitality, William and George returned to Antonio María Lugo's ranch and brought their men back to the mission. Over the next two weeks, William became good friends with Father Sánchez, who showed William his vineyards and orchards where an abundance of fruit was being grown.[88] William learned that this land had been turned into a garden through an extensive irrigation system and hard work. Once certain he would return to Santa Fe, William now felt intrigued by California, where the land was fertile and a man could start a new life. His spirit of adventure had always driven him forward, but perhaps he could finally put down his roots in this new frontier.

~

PERSONAL OBSERVATIONS AND RESEARCH

In late 1830-1831, William Wolfskill, a trail blazer, led one of the early expeditions over much of the Main Route of the Old Spanish Trail,[89] also known as the Northern Route. The Wolfskill expedition started out from Abiquiu, New Mexico, traveled into southwestern Colorado near present-day Durango, north to the Green River area, across to Castle Dale and down through central Utah. After going through eastern Nevada, the expedition then crossed into California where they traveled on the Mojave Indian trails, over the Cajon Pass and finally arrived in Los Angeles. Called the "longest, crookedest, most arduous pack mule route in the history of America,"[90] the Old Spanish Trail served as an important trade route mainly from 1829 until the late 1840s.

Leaving in late September of 1830, William and his group of between 17 to 20 fellow trappers arrived in San Gabriel, California, in February of 1831 after four and a half months of travel through dangerous, rugged terrain, sometimes with little water and food. As the leader of the expedition, William hired 11 trappers and was joined by his friend from Missouri, George Yount, who brought along several more men. There were also several free trappers.[91] The number of people in this group has been the object of speculation since William did not keep a journal during the trip. The only document that survived this expedition is a ledger of all the sales and payments for transactions that William recorded during the years of 1830-1832. The original ledger is still in the Wolfskill family and a copy also resides in the Huntington Library in San Marino, California. In his ledger, 17 men are shown to have bought items from William as they traveled from New Mexico to California.[92] However, Ziba Branch, a trapper on the expedition, reported years later that there were 21 trappers.[93]

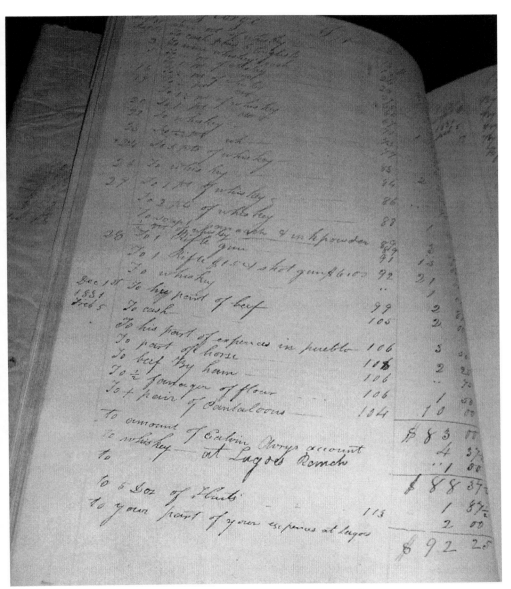

Page from Original 1830-1832 Ledger

Courtesy of Linda Wolfskill Pawinski

Except for William's ledger, there are no diaries or documents that were written at the time of the actual expedition. Hence, my source materials include several accounts written years later by people who interviewed some of the expedition members. The most comprehensive account is in *George C. Yount and his Chronicles of the West*, a series of recollections Yount dictated to his friend, the Reverend Orange Clark, who wrote them up in 1855.[94] Fellow trapper, Ziba Branch related his memory of the trip that was published in 1859. H.D. Barrows also gave several short summaries of the historic journey based on William's recollections long after the trip. Because these accounts were recorded years after the Wolfskill expedition, we have a good idea of the general course of their journey but do not know their exact route.

Inspired after reading these various accounts, Rich and I decided to learn everything we could about the Old Spanish Trail, which is actually a network of trails ranging over 2800 miles.[95] Since the terrain was too rough, there were no wagon caravans so traders traveled in pack mule trains. A flourishing trade grew with New Mexican merchants who exchanged their thick woolen blankets and other woven items for cheap California horses and mules.

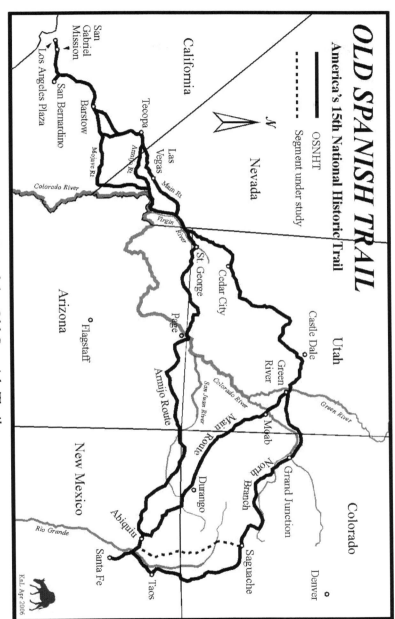

Map of the Old Spanish Trail
Courtesy of the Old Spanish Trail Association

The Old Spanish Trail is made up of four major trails as well as a number of smaller alternate trails:

1) **The Main Route also known as the Northern Route**: Traveled over by the Wolfskill expedition early on, this route was long and circuitous. George Yount had been through this area before on Native American trails and was familiar with the Ute lands and Mojave villages, which was helpful as William led his expedition into this relatively unknown territory.[96] Later favored by traders and trappers, the Main Route/Northern Route[97] started off from Abiquiu or Santa Fe, crossed into southwestern Colorado, continued into Utah, up through Moab, over to Castle Dale, down central Utah and through the present-day Cedar City area. After leaving southern Utah, it went through Nevada, entered into California, crossed over the Cajon Pass and finished the journey to Los Angeles, California.

2) **The Armijo Route**: In 1829, Antonio Armijo and his caravan of 60 traders and 100 mules were the first to travel from Abiquiu, New Mexico, to Los Angeles on one of the main routes of the Old Spanish Trail.[98] They followed a more direct route through northern Arizona and southern Utah where they retraced part of the same area covered by the Domínguez-Escalante Party 53 years earlier.[99] They continued into Nevada, entered California, crossed over the Cajon Pass and on to the San Gabriel Mission. However, the Armijo Route was not widely used by later expeditions since the trail was very difficult to navigate for both traders and animals[100] as well as there being serious hostilities between trappers and several Native American tribes in the Arizona part of the route.[101]

3) **The North Branch**: This route followed trapper and Native American trails from Santa Fe and Taos, New Mexico, into Colorado, through the Gunnison National Forest, crossing through present-day Grand Junction and eventually joining up with the Main Route/ Northern Route around present-day Green River, Utah.

4) **The Mojave Route**: The Old Spanish Trail followed the ancient Mojave Indian trails that crossed the Mojave Desert in California and provided a connection between the Mojave villages on the Colorado River and the California coast.[102] William traveled on the Indian trails after he left the Mojave Indian villages and headed to the small town of *El Pueblo de Los Angeles*.

Rich and I have traveled over most of the different routes of the Old Spanish Trail in order to understand what William Wolfskill experienced on his trailblazing expedition. We also joined the Old Spanish Trail Association (OSTA) made up of historians, history lovers, genealogists and trail experts who shared their knowledge with us during our research. We have found the OSTA conferences a great way to learn about the Trail.

On our first trip in 2008, we started from our home in Los Angeles, the city at the end of the Old Spanish Trail, crossed over the Cajon Pass in California and drove on to Las Vegas, Nevada. Instead of slot machines and jackpots, we were looking for the watering holes where travelers on the Old Spanish Trail would have rested after passing through the hot Nevada desert. Driving past casinos and down wide boulevards, it was hard to imagine that artesian springs once made this area an oasis of green pastures, hence the name Las Vegas meaning "fertile plain or meadows" in Spanish. When we arrived at the Springs Preserve about three miles from downtown Las Vegas, dozens of school children were streaming out of their school buses. They soon learned how the springs provided water over the centuries for the local Native Americans and later for the Old Spanish Trail travelers. William missed these plentiful springs of Las Vegas since his journey took him further east down the Virgin River to the Colorado River, then south to the present-day Searchlight area in Nevada on his way to California.

Later, Rich and I followed the Trail northeast to Cedar City, Utah, where Al Matheson, an expert on the Old Spanish Trail, and his wife, Barbara, took us to Braffits Canyon, an area close to Summit, Utah, where William and his group most likely camped.[103] Al grew up in Cedar City and learned much about the Trail from his father, Alva Matheson. We traveled caravan-style in our SUVs up the canyon on a well-maintained dirt road, which turned into a rocky, rough pathway. When the road became impassable, we pulled over and parked. After walking through sagebrush, cacti and scrub cedar trees, we crossed a riverbed and kept climbing. At a precipitous ledge, I dug my shoes into the dirt and gripped a tree branch so I wouldn't fall down the hill. We made our way through low-lying bushes and arrived at a flat area encircled by small boulders where Al Matheson thinks William Wolfskill and his group may have camped. We sat down on large rocks and listened to the wind as it rustled through the trees and up the canyon. I could imagine William kneeling on the ground to start up a campfire after a long day on the trail.

Al took us further up the canyon to show us a boulder with inscriptions that may date from the Wolfskill expedition. It is inscribed with the numbers 1831 and the word Gold in capital letters—the letters G and L are written backwards. Al told us that fortune hunters, drawn by the hope of discovering gold, had dynamited the boulder years ago but did not find any gold. On the boulder, there are several letters of the alphabet including the two letters that look like **I** and **W**. Steve Heath, a former President of the Old Spanish Trail Association, has studied early trapper rock inscriptions. Since William was known in New Mexico as José Guillermo Wolfskill or Joseph William Wolfskill, Heath theorizes that the **I** and **W** could actually stand for José or Joseph Wolfskill since the letter **I** was used by the some of the early travelers to signify **J** and that in old Spanish the letter **J** was often a variation of the letter **I**. Heath further cites the inscription of May 3, 1836, on the side of a canyon along the Green River, by trapper Denis Julien, who used a symbol very similar to the letter **I** when he spelled Julien. Heath points out that Braffits Canyon would have been one of the few places where William's expedition could have crossed over the mountains after experiencing the terrible snow storm in the Panguitch area.

When Al Matheson showed us the boulder, it was an exciting discovery. In the middle of this isolated wilderness, I was astounded to see what could be perhaps a message from William's expedition as they made their way through this craggy and remote landscape. In 2016, Al took us to see the boulder again which still survives among the lava rocks on the mountain. We are hopeful that it will get some historical recognition as part of the Wolfskill expedition.

Wolfskill Boulder with 1831 Inscription and
Conchita Thornton Marusich
Photo by Richard Marusich

Close Up of 1831 Inscription on Wolfskill Boulder
Photo by Richard Marusich

Our next stop in 2008 was the Castle Dale area in Utah described by George Yount as "repulsive and supremely awful."[104] Rich and I spent three hours crossing the dustiest and most desolate backcountry area. There were no signs or cars so we were not even sure that we were on the right road until a weather-beaten sign miraculously appeared on the side of the dirt road marking the Old Spanish Trail. We kept driving and found several other small, white Old Spanish Trail signs that pointed us in the right direction and saved us when we encountered badly marked forks in the road. We both wondered how William and his band made it out of this forsaken place. At least, we had the Old Spanish Trail signs to guide us. When we arrived at U.S. Highway 6, our car had been transformed from silver to brown, and our mouths and skin felt gritty with trail dust. On our return trip in 2016, we found the road had been vastly improved but traveling over the area was still quite an adventure.

Old Spanish Trail Sign on Road in Castle Dale
Photo by Conchita Thornton Marusich

On the Trail in Castle Dale, Utah
Photo by Conchita Thornton Marusich

Still in Utah, we drove through stunning red cliff canyons on Utah State Route 128 as we searched for the point where the Colorado and Dolores rivers join, which H.D. Barrows mentioned in his account of Wolfskill's historic journey.[105] The confluence of the Colorado and Dolores rivers can be found about a mile up from the Dewey Bridge driving north on Route 128 towards Interstate 70 on the right-hand side of the road.

In his *Chronicles of the West*, George Yount described the funeral of a Ute chief encountered by the Wolfskill expedition on the Old Spanish Trail. To learn more about the Utes, in 2008 we visited a small museum on the reservation in Ignacio, Colorado, dedicated to preserving the Ute tribe's culture and history. We entered the exhibit to the sound of rhythmic chants and admired exquisite quill and bead work on deerskin clothing. We found out that a group from the Ute tribe had just returned from a trip on horseback with some of the tribal elders who remembered what their parents had told them about the Old Spanish Trail.

I also learned that the traders who traveled over the Old Spanish Trail had followed a network of older trails established by various Native American tribes including the Utes. Several years after our initial visit, the Ute tribe built a beautiful new museum nearby called the Southern Ute Cultural Center and Museum in Ignacio, Colorado, which we have visited several times to learn more about the Ute culture.

When we reached Abiquiu, New Mexico, our final destination, we stood in the main plaza feeling profound respect for the bravery and fearlessness of William and his crew of trappers. Abiquiu has a timeless quality that offered us a glimpse of what William might have seen in his day. The dirt and gravel roads were bordered with adobe buildings. On one corner a crumbling adobe home with exposed wooden beams hinted at the roof that once rested on its walls. I wondered if William and his group saw the old building as they rode north out of town in September 1830, heading towards California.

After exploring the little town, Rich and I bought green chili chicken stew at Bode's General Store, drove to the outskirts of Abiquiu and sat beside the Chama River which glistened like thousands of diamonds in the afternoon sun. We had covered the entire trail and were in awe of William and the other trappers whose tenacity and courage gave them the strength to endure more than four months of hardship after hardship. Sitting beside the Chama River, we raised our glasses filled with fine New Mexico wine and toasted William Wolfskill's courage in undertaking such a trip and imagined him leading his group of trappers north away from Abiquiu.

Chama River Near Abiquiu, New Mexico
Photo by Conchita Thornton Marusich

63 Camp, ed., *George C. Yount and his Chronicles of the West* (Denver: Old West Publishing Company, 1966), 85.
64 Russell, *Journal of a Trapper*, 82. Osborne Russell gives a lengthy description of a trapper's clothing.
65 Mrs. F.H. Day, "Ziba Branch," *The Hesperian*, Vol.III, (October: 1859): 338.
66 Hafen and Hafen, *Old Spanish Trail* (Glendale: Arthur H. Clark Company, 1954), 145.
67 Ibid, 145. And Wolfskill Ledger.
68 Camp, ed., *George C. Yount and his Chronicles of the West*, 14.
69 Barrows, "The Story of an Old Pioneer."
70 In Yount's recollection, it is unclear where the expedition's encounter with the Ute funeral took place. Charles Camp who edited Yount's Chronicles thought that the Ute funeral took place around the Green River area early on in the trip since Yount talked about the Ute funeral before he spoke about St Joseph's Valley and Pleasant Valley, 262.

71 Since George Yount had traveled through the Ute lands a number of times before he joined the Wolfskill expedition, it appears that George spoke at least some basic Ute language. At the Chief's funeral, he seemed to communicate well with the Utes.

72 Camp, ed., *George C. Yount and his Chronicles of the West*, 86.

73 Ibid., 86-87. This is a direct quote from the *Chronicles*.

74 Ibid., 87.

75 Ibid.

76 Ibid.

77 Ibid., 87-88. There is some confusion where this part of the story took place. Though Yount referred to this region as St Joseph's Valley in the narrative, Charles Camp, the editor, felt that Yount was referring to the barren desert east of the Castle Dale region in this section, 262.

78 Ibid., 88. Charles Camp, the editor, wrote that Pleasant Valley could have been located in an upper valley of the Sevier River, 262.

79 Ibid., 88-89.

80 Harold Austin Steiner, *The Old Spanish Trail: Across the Mojave Desert* (Las Vegas, Nevada: The Haldor Company, 1999), 46.

81 Camp, ed., *George C. Yount and his Chronicles of the West*, 90.

82 Ibid., 91.

83 Day, "Ziba Branch," 338. Ziba remembered that the last ox was killed near Little Salt Lake, a seasonal lake located west of present-day Paragonah and Interstate 15. Others doubt this occurred at this location, questioning whether an ox could have survived the terrible snow storm that the Wolfskill expedition had just experienced in the mountains near Panguitch, Utah.

84 Camp, ed., *C. Yount and his Chronicles of the West*, 93.

85 Day, "Ziba Branch," 338.

86 Wolfskill. "Ledger of Accounts, 1830-1832." On George Yount's page in the Wolfskill ledger, it is written that the expedition arrived at the Lugo Ranch on February 5, 1831. This may have been Lugo's *Rancho San Antonio* which he was granted in 1810.

87 Camp, ed., *C. Yount and his Chronicles of the West*, 94-96.

88 Ibid., 97.

89 LeRoy Hafen and Ann W. Hafen, *Old Spanish Trail*, 139.

90 Ibid., 19.

91 Ibid., 141-142.

92 William Wolfskill Ledger, "Ledger of Accounts, 1830-1832," Huntington Library, (San Marino, CA.) Hafen and Hafen, *Old Spanish Trail*, 141. According to William Wolfskill's ledger, there were 17 names of men who bought items from Wolfskill while they traveled from late September of 1830 to February of 1831. Their names are: "John Lewis, Zachariah Ham, David Keller, Ziba Branch, Alexander Branch, Francisco Lafurry (Le Fourri), Sangerma (Baptiste St. Germain), Samuel Shields, John Ray (Rhea), José Archulate (Archuleta), George Yount, Blass Greago, Garry (Guerra), Manuel Mondragon, Love Hardisty, Martin Cooper, and Lewis Burton."

93 Mrs. F.H. Day, "Ziba Branch," *The Hesperian*, 338. Ziba Branch was also known as Francis Ziba Branch.

94 Camp, ed., *C. Yount and his Chronicles of the West*, xvii.

95 http://www.oldspanishtrail.org/learn/faqs.php

96 LeRoy Hafen and Ann W. Hafen, *Old Spanish Trail*, 140,141.

97 This route is called both the Main Route and the Northern Route. The Old Spanish Trail Association members tend to use the term Main Route while the National Park Service, BLM and the United States Department of the Interior refer to it as the Northern Route in their documents and maps. This route was used so frequently by the traders and travelers that it became the main route of the Old Spanish Trail.

98 Elizabeth von Till Warren, "The Old Spanish National Historic Trail," http://www. oldspanishtrail.org/learn/trail_history.php

99 Hafen and Hafen, *Old Spanish Trail*, 165-166.

100 Steiner, *The Old Spanish Trail: Across the Mojave Desert*, 44-46.

101 Hafen and Hafen, *Old Spanish Trail*, 131.

102 Dennis G. Casebier, *Mojave Road Guide: An Adventure Through Time* (Essex, California: Tales of the Mojave Road Publishing Company, 2010), 17.

103 Hafen and Hafen, *Old Spanish Trail*, 147. In 1951, Hafen visited Braffits Canyon but called it Winn's Canyon where he saw the Wolfskill Boulder with its rock inscriptions.

104 Camp, ed., *George C. Yount and his Chronicles of the West*, 88.

105 Barrows, "The Story of an Old Pioneer," *Wilmington Journal*.

CHAPTER 6

BLACK STAR CANYON HORSE THIEVES

William's Story and Personal Observations

A Wolfskill cousin recently called to tell me that a "haunted tour" in Orange County, California was advertised on the internet with the following teaser: "By lantern light, follow the ghost of William Wolfskill up Black Star Canyon where he massacred an entire Indian village." I have read many accounts about William Wolfskill and never encountered anything suggesting that he killed an entire village. I set out to get to the bottom of this claim. First, I spoke with the naturalist who led the haunted tour. He informed me he based his information on accounts by local historians, including Terry Stephenson, who relied on an account by William Wolfskill's ranch foreman, Joseph Edward Pleasants, also known as J.E. Pleasants.

In his book, *Shadows of Old Saddleback: Tales of the Santa Ana Mountains*, published in 1931, Orange County historian, Terry Stephenson, wrote that William Wolfskill and his trappers, fresh off the Old Spanish Trail in early 1831, agreed to go after some Indian horse thieves who had been stealing horses from local ranchers. Stephenson maintained he was repeating what William Wolfskill had recounted to J.E. Pleasants 70 years earlier.[106]

Since a massacre of an entire Indian village does not seem in character for my great-great-grandfather, I wanted to go back to the original source and verify if J.E. Pleasants had written anything about William's pursuit of the horse thieves. The University of California,

Irvine has a vast collection of letters and writings by Pleasants who chronicled early California life and was published in various magazines and newspapers. Rich and I culled through numerous boxes reading published as well as unpublished material, but finding nothing. We were getting discouraged when Rich, in an excited whisper (since we were in a library) said, "I think I've found the story." Titled "Wolfskill Indian Raid" and handwritten on two and a half pages, J.E. Pleasants described the story in the following way:

Wm Wolfskill [was] heading a party of about 20 trappers which arrived in January of 1831 from Taos, New Mexico. Among the men were Branch, Burton, Shields, Ham and Cooper who settled in the West, most of them in California. The rancheros around L.A. had been losing horses for some time by the raids of the desert Indians who by stealth drove off the animals taking them through the mountain cañóns[107] and eventually working them through the mountain passes on to the desert where they used them for food, horse flesh being much more prized by them than beef. The newcomers of the Wolfskill party being well armed and ready for adventure were employed by the rancheros to pursue the Indians and try to reclaim the stolen stock. They followed a trail picked up on one of the outlying ranches and followed it to the mountains lying east of the Santa Ana Valley. Following up the Santiago cañón some 8 miles from the valley, they tracked the driven animals to a cañón which branches off from the main cañón to the north...[108]

The writing stopped mid-page with no further details on the story. Rich and I continued to look for the rest of the account among his notes and manuscripts to no avail. We could not find any corroboration of the Indian massacre.

In his book, *Shadows of Old Saddleback*, Stephenson describes how the trappers traveled deep into the canyon and surprised the horse thieves, killing several of them and retrieving the stolen horses.[109] However, there is no mention of a massacre of an Indian village nor is there any mention that William personally killed any of the horse thieves. So, after our research, we concluded that William and the trappers may have gone after them but that the massacre is based on hearsay. There is no written account of the whole event and Pleasants, who would have been quite elderly when telling the story to Stephenson, also could have dramatized the end. In any case, we will never know the definitive story unless the full version of the event as recalled by Pleasants is found.

Intrigued by William's chase after the horse thieves, Rich and I drove to Black Star Canyon, which is now part of the Orange County Parks system. A narrow dirt road through the steep canyon was open to hikers but not to car traffic except for property owners in the area. We were hoping to see Hidden Ranch where the alleged showdown occurred between Wolfskill's group and the horse thieves but were discouraged when we heard Hidden Ranch is about eight miles up the Canyon. A local ranger offered to drive us as far as the road was passable so off we went through oaks and sycamores with coastal sage and black sage on either side of the dirt road.

Black Star Canyon in Orange County
Photo by Conchita Thornton Marusich

Undeveloped except for an occasional ranch, the rugged land is similar to what William would have seen in 1831. It is hard for me to imagine William and his group gunning down the horse thieves. But it was a different time when people on the western frontier often took the law into their own hands, and the principle "innocent until proven guilty" was rarely applied in disputes. What I do know is that on the Santa Fe Trail and the Old Spanish Trail where William had several encounters with different Indian tribes, which could have turned violent, historians have never reported any such behavior on the part of William Wolfskill.

---

106 Terry E. Stephenson, *Shadows of Old Saddleback: Tales of the Santa Ana Mountains* (Orange, California: The Rasmussen Press, 1974), 105-106.

107 J.E. Pleasants uses the Spanish word "cañón" to mean "canyon" throughout his "Wolfskill Indian Raid" story.

108 J.E. Pleasants "Wolfskill Indian Raid," J.E. Pleasants Papers, Special Collections and Archives, UC Irvine Libraries. These two and a half handwritten pages are unpublished notes by J.E. Pleasants that are the only evidence of this story that we could find.

109 Stephenson, *Shadows of Old Saddleback: Tales of the Santa Ana Mountains*, 105-106.

CHAPTER 7

ARRIVING IN EL PUEBLO DE LOS ANGELES

William's Story

After paying off his men for their work during the journey over the Old Spanish Trail, William arrived in the small, Mexican town of *El Pueblo de Los Angeles* in 1831, almost penniless. He had hoped to re-join Ewing Young in the Tulare and Sacramento areas in California where they had planned to go beaver trapping. However, Ewing had already returned to Santa Fe.

Being a practical man, William heard there was money to be made from hunting sea otter. Under Mexican law, he needed a license but the authorities were very strict only allowing Mexican citizens to receive permits. Undaunted, William decided to approach the authorities.

"My name is Guillermo Wolfskill. I'm here to apply for a license to hunt sea otters. Here's my permit issued by the governor of New Mexico."[110]

William dug into his pouch and produced the permit. The document gave William the right to hunt for "*nutria*" the Spanish word used in California for "sea otter." What William neglected to mention was that the word "*nutria*" was used in New Mexico to mean "beaver." So even though his permit was for beaver trapping, William was hoping to take advantage of the word mix-up.

The official read the document several times and stated,

"I see that you are authorized to hunt for "*nutria*" however in California only Mexican citizens are allowed to do so."

"I am a Mexican citizen." William showed his citizenship papers.

He thought back to the time in Taos, New Mexico, when he had applied to be a Mexican citizen on March 25, 1830.[111] He remembered feeling nervous the day of his petition hearing because he would have to convince the members of the *Ayuntamiento de Taos*, the town council, that he was serious about becoming a Mexican citizen. His two friends, Juan de los Reyes Martínez and Antonio Lucero, had signed his petition confirming that William had been baptized Catholic and that he was in good standing with the local parish.

William waited while the council members debated his petition. Would they accept this foreign trapper or would they turn him away as an intruder from Missouri? Would they understand that even though he was not a native son, he had learned their language, joined their church and felt at home in their country? He had written in his petition:

"...I promise to uphold the constitution or constitutional laws, and the general laws of the United Mexican States..."

William remembered waiting outside for the verdict when an official from the Taos *Ayuntamiento* approached him.

"José Guillermo Wolfskill. Your petition was considered. We were debating whether or not you were truly serious in becoming a Catholic."

The official then smiled.

"The local priest 'verified' your conversion. Therefore, we have approved your petition. We will now send this petition on to the governor so that he can issue you a letter of naturalization. *Felicitaciones* [congratulations] on becoming a Mexican citizen."[112]

When the Taos *Ayuntamiento* or Town Council approved his request for naturalization, they wrote: "It is well known that the manner in which he has conducted himself is well respected and admired politically, religiously and in civil matters."[113] It was a bittersweet moment since William knew he loved his new country but would always retain a strong feeling for his family home in Missouri.

Now William was facing this official in *El Pueblo de Los Angeles* who seemed to doubt his citizenship papers and his right to hunt *nutria*. The official started to squirm, reading the documents in front of him several times before he announced,

"Well, I suppose we must honor this authorization."

The Governor of California, Manuel Victoria, did not agree and informed Vicente Sánchez, the mayor of Los Angeles, "*Guillermo Wolfskill no debe pescar en California sino en Sonora donde obtuvo licencia*" ["William Wolfskill should not fish in California but in Sonora where he obtained the license"].[114] However, William's good friend, Father Sánchez from the San Gabriel Mission, intervened on his behalf.

With his trapping permit accepted by the local Mexican authorities, William and several partners, set out to build a schooner to hunt for sea otter. They hired a young carpenter originally from Massachusetts called José or Joseph Chapman who worked for Father Sánchez at the mission. The colorful Yankee had landed in California in 1818 while in the service of an Argentinean pirate named Hippolyte Bouchard. After terrorizing settlements and missions along the coast of Alta California, Bouchard's two ships and hundreds of pirates sailed away but Chapman stayed on in Alta California[115] and became a Mexican citizen. Because Chapman had served as an apprentice under a master shipbuilder in Boston, William and several partners hired him to build a schooner they would call the *Refugio* with wood from the local mountains. The lumber was cut and delivered to San Gabriel in wooden carts where it was assembled. Weighing 60 tons and measuring 70 feet long, the ship was disassembled and taken to the San Pedro harbor where it was rebuilt in 1831.[116] Wolfskill and his crew first set sail for Baja California going south to Cedros Island in January of 1832 and eventually north to the waters off San Luis Obispo where they continued to search for sea otter. Wolfskill and his partners had little luck and decided to sell the *Refugio* to a sea captain named Hinckley.[117] This concluded William's brief career as a sea otter hunter.

Instead of returning to New Mexico, William decided to stay in *El Pueblo de Los Angeles*. In 1833, he acquired a small piece of land between present-day Spring and New High streets where he could grow grapes and build a home near the old plaza church that stood on the main square. He settled down with María de la Luz Valencia, his common-law wife, and her daughters Manuela and Petra Valencia.[118] William and María de la Luz's first child together, María Susana, was baptized on November 18, 1833, at the Church of Our Lady or *La Igelsia de Nuestra Señora* located on the plaza.[119] Their son, Timoteo, was baptized in the same church on January 30, 1835.[120]

In January of 1836, the Los Angeles City Council or *Ayunatamiento* decided that it was "necessary" to count all the residents of the pueblo in a General Register and appointed a committee under the direction of the city attorney to carry this out. At its January 14 meeting, the committee reported they were busy at work collecting the information with "all possible diligence."[121] The Wolfskill household was entered as follows in the City of Los Angeles Register: William, a "laborer," was listed along with Luz Valencia, Man'la Valencia Wolfskill (an abbreviation for Manuela), Timoteo Valencia Wolfskill (though they called him Juan in error) and Susana Valencia Wolfskill.[122]

William was working as a carpenter to support his family. Back in Missouri, the Wolfskill family had built everything they needed to survive on the frontier, which had given William experience in carpentry. He also was learning about growing grapes and making wine—in fact, he loved the taste of a good brandy or *aguardiente*. He expanded his land holdings and planted more grape vines.

In April 1836, a dark cloud gathered over the pueblo as Los Angeles was gripped with fury over the murder of Domingo Felix, a *ranchero* who had mysteriously been found dead.[123] Although there were no witnesses, everyone was convinced that his wife's lover, Gervacio

Alipáz, a 36-year-old, cowboy or *vaquero*, had killed Domingo. María del Rosario Villa Felix, Domingo's wife, and Gervacio had been living together for two years while Domingo had tried in vain to force María back into their marriage. In desperation, María fled to the protection of the San Gabriel Mission where she had been baptized. Domingo followed and demanded that his wife return to their *rancho* with him. The priests encouraged María to reconcile with her husband and she relented. Victorious in reclaiming his wife, a triumphant Domingo and dejected María were riding back to the *rancho* when Gervacio reportedly ambushed Domingo in an arroyo, lassoed and dragged him from his horse, killing him with a knife. The story was told that María had assisted in covering up the body with leaves and dirt.[124]

Now the pueblo sought vengeance. There were rumors that María's husband had been unfaithful which may have caused her to look elsewhere for love.[125] But this brought no pity from the people of the pueblo; they stood determined that she and Alipáz needed to die in order to serve as an example for others. There was also great concern that justice would be delayed until the courts in Mexico ruled on the couple's punishment. The idea that the lovers could go free during a long delay or even be pardoned by the new, incoming governor was too outrageous.

On April 7, 1836, an agitated mob gathered at the home of John Temple, a leading merchant in the pueblo who was related to the mur-dered Domingo Felix through his wife, Rafaela Cota. Calling them-selves the Defenders of the Public Safety, the group, led by Victor Prudon, wrote up their grievances.[126] William Wolfskill was there with neighbors and friends including Jean Louis Vignes and Francisco Araujo. All three men signed their names to the passionate ultima-tum, as did 52 other leading citizens.[127] The feeling in the room that day was that the couple's guilt was so clear that a trial was unnecessary. María's youth, her husband Domingo's possible infidelity and the need to substantiate the crime were forgotten in the passion of the moment.

The Defenders sent a signed petition over to the *ayuntamiento*, which was meeting that day:

> The undersigned citizens summoned to meet by the rest of the citizens of this jurisdiction who are justly indignant at the horrible crime committed on the person of the late Domingo Feliz…ask you to execute or deliver to us for immediate execution, the assassin Gervacio Alipáz and the unfaithful María del Rosario Villa, his accomplice, this abominable monstrosity, who sacrificed her husband, that she might enjoy the immoral appetite which she craved for. Nature trembles at the sight of this venomous reptile, and the soil turns barren in its refusal to support these detestable existences. Let this infernal pair perish. It is the will of the people. We shall not lay down our arms while our petition is not granted and the murderers not executed. The proof of their guilt is so clear that justice needs no investigation. The public requires an example and also revenge, and must be satisfied…We swear that the public will be avenged today, or die in the attempt. The blood of the murderers must be shed today, or ours will, until the last drop…[128]

The Defenders of the Public Safety gave the city council one hour to make their decision and ended their petition stating:

> If in that time no answer has been received, then the judges will be responsible before God and the public of what might follow. Death to the murderer![129]

The council members responded by inviting Victor Prudon, the leader of the Defenders to address the council. Prudon not only declined the invitation but sent a message asking for either the execution of the prisoners or the key to the dwelling where María del

Rosario was being held. Manuel Requena, council president, wrote a note back that the owner of the dwelling was instructed not to let anyone have access to María, adding "The prisoner is left there at the disposition of the law only. God and Liberty."[130] But in reality, the council members felt at a loss to stop the crowd from lynching the prisoners because there were too few guards to control the mob.

Since the city council showed no inclination to hand over the prisoners, the Defenders took the law into their own hands and decided that the execution must proceed. It was reported that Alipáz had almost filed off his shackles when the vigilante group arrived at his cell. The angry mob shot him and María near the house of Abel Stearns, one of the pueblo's leading citizens.[131] Their bodies were laid out in front of the jail for two hours so that everyone could view the executed couple.[132] The Defenders of the Public Safety sent back the following note to the city council:

> The dead bodies of Gervacio Alipás and María del Rosario Villa are at your disposal for burial. We also forward you the jail keys that you may deliver them to whomsoever is on guard. In case you are in need of men to serve as guards, we are all at your disposal.[133]

When the new governor, Mariano Chico, arrived in California in April of 1836, he was furious with the Defenders of the Public Safety and arrested Victor Prudon along with other top members of the group, threatening to execute them.[134] They were all later released and the Defenders disbanded.

The fury that had consumed the pueblo receded and life returned to its slow pace. Meanwhile, Luz Valencia, who was pregnant, informed William that she and Manuela were leaving.[135] After her son, José de la Cruz Valencia, was born, Luz baptized him on

June 3, 1836, but she did not list William as the father. Instead the baptismal record noted that the father was "unknown" or "*no conocido*."[136] Within a month, Luz married William's neighbor, Francisco Araujo, a silversmith, on July 1, 1836, at the San Gabriel Mission.[137] It was written in the margin of José de la Cruz Valencia's baptismal record that Luz married Francisco Araujo in order to "legitimize" her son.[138] Luz had left Susana and Timoteo with William so he was now both father and mother to their two children.

One night in 1837, William sat down to write to his family in Missouri. By candlelight, he took out a bottle of ink he had just bought from a trade ship recently arrived from San Diego. He selected a quill, sharpened it with his favorite knife, and upon carefully dipping his quill into the ink, was ready to put his thoughts down on paper.

"Dear Family," he wrote.

Not knowing how to begin, he thought about what had happened. How could he explain that Luz had left him, given birth to a son who was possibly fathered by another man and had ultimately married his neighbor? He thought about how Francisco Araujo had been forced to leave the pueblo in 1837 by order of Governor Carlos Antonio Carrillo and that Luz had gone to Mexico with him. Then came the news that Francisco Araujo had been killed in Mazatlán, Mexico, in a dispute over Luz.[139]

As William watched the sputtering candle flame, he put down his quill and let out a deep sigh. He looked at the fire in the hearth and tore up the unfinished letter. He would never send a letter to worry his family but just getting his thoughts together helped lift the burden from his heart. He tossed the pieces of his letter into the flames.

Personal Observations and Research

When I decided to search for William Wolfskill's legacy in Los Angeles, my initial focus was on the area where he first lived after arriving from the Old Spanish Trail in 1831. At that time *El Pueblo de Los Angeles* was a small Mexican settlement of adobe houses and dirt streets clustered around the main plaza and inhabited by *Californios*, members of the Gabrielino tribe, traders, former mountain men and foreigners. The *Californios* were people of Spanish or Mexican descent who were born in Alta California when it was under Spain and later Mexico. Spanish was primarily spoken in the pueblo although other languages such as English and French were heard on a daily basis.

The Gabrielino Indians, also known as the Kizh, the Tongva and the San Gabriel Band of Mission Indians, had made this land their home for thousands of years before the founding of *El Pueblo de Los Angeles* in 1781 under Spanish rule. That year Governor Felipe de Neve began preparations to start a settlement near the Los Angeles River. As he drew up a plan for the new town, he waited for the arrival of the settlers and soldiers, which included 11 families or 44 men, women and children[140] mainly from Sinaloa, Mexico. When they arrived, they were a racially diverse group of Spaniards, Indians, *mestizos*[141], mulattos[142] and blacks. Each family was given land to farm near the plaza and over time the town grew from this group of settlers.

Through my genealogical research, I discovered that I am descended from Francisco Salvador Lugo, one of four soldiers who escorted these settlers from the San Gabriel Mission to the plaza[143] and their new farmland. September 4, 1781, is the official date of this journey of the initial *pobladores* or townspeople, which commemorates the founding of the pueblo. However, the process most likely occurred over a period of months as many settlers received their land in the plaza area between June and August of 1781.[144] Lugo was a soldier from Sinaloa, Mexico, and had been recruited to take part in the settlement of Alta or Upper

California with his wife, Juana María Rita Vianazul Martínez, and several children.[145] We will meet more Lugos again later on in William's story.

By 1831, when William Wolfskill arrived after his long journey over the Old Spanish Trail, the population of *El Pueblo de Los Angeles* had grown from the initial 44 settlers to approximately 1400 people.[146] To discover my roots, Rich and I researched where William had lived in order to understand what connections to him still exist in the City of Angels. We found an 1887 map of the downtown area, which prompted us to visit New High and Spring Streets, the site of William's first house. We were lucky to find the area in present-day Chinatown since many of the original streets have either been renamed or lost through development. As we drove through Chinatown, I tried visualizing William's adobe house that would have been built in a cluster of other adobes near the church on the square, quite a contrast to the strip malls and Chinese restaurants that fill New High Street today. We drove a few more blocks and arrived at Olvera Street, a vibrant, bustling street near Chinatown, still filled with remnants of its old Mexican heritage including the historic Avila Adobe. Built in 1818, this little gem is the oldest existing house in Los Angeles.

Walking down Olvera Street, we passed by a collection of Mexican restaurants and outdoor stalls selling Mexican trinkets. The sounds of Mariachi music and the pungent smells of *carnitas* and *barbacoa* filled the air as we caught sight of the Avila Adobe where we hoped to connect to early California history.

The whitewashed Avila Adobe catapulted us back in time when several docents wearing long skirts and shawls invited us to join their tour about the Avila family in the 1840s. The piano in the parlor or *la sala* reminded me of my mother's story that William Wolfskill had shipped a piano around Cape Horn, located at the tip of South America, so that his family could enjoy music. The adobe's kitchen or *cocina* with its stone *metate* for grinding corn and its corner fireplace would have produced many family dinners.

Avila Adobe Parlor
Photo by Richard Marusich Used with Permission
from El Pueblo Historical Monument

Avila Adobe Kitchen
Photo by Richard Marusich Used with Permission
from El Pueblo Historical Monument

Rich and I continued to the courtyard where I remembered the wonderful birthday party we gave my mother at the Avila Adobe on September 20, 2001, for her 87th birthday. We received special permission to have the party there because my mother had been the Queen of Los Angeles on September 4, 1941. She had ended her reign-for-the-day at the Avila Adobe by cutting cake in celebration of Los Angeles' 160th birthday. Mama had been chosen Queen because she was a talented actress as well as a descendant from the early *Californio* families of the Lugos from Santa Barbara, the Juarez family from Napa and Santa Barbara as well as the Estudillos and de Pedrorenas from San Diego. The pride my mother had in our Latino heritage filled me as we sat in that peaceful outdoor courtyard surrounded by the visions of early California days.

ELENA WOLFSKILL, queen of the allday celebration, shown cutting piece of birthday cake for little Nina Gage.

Elena Wolfskill Cutting Cake at Avila Adobe on September 4, 1941
Courtesy of Elena Wolfskill Thornton

Further research on early Los Angeles led me in a different direction where I learned about the dark side of life in the pueblo. Alta California had been under Mexican rule and laws since 1821 when Mexico won its independence from Spain. Yet it was so far from the leadership hub of Mexico City that Alta California suffered from long delays in communication from the Mexican government and uneven administration of justice. The daily governance of the pueblo depended on the wisdom and cooperation of its inhabitants as they put those laws into effect. I learned what happens when mob mentality sweeps a town and destroys the thin veneer of a civil society.

In continuing my research, I discovered information about Luz Valencia, William's common-law wife. Not much is known about Luz who had two children, María Susana and Timoteo, with William. One of my main sources was the Early California Population Project, an online database compiled by the Huntington Library in San Marino, California. This is an important resource for genealogists and others wanting to research descendants from early California since the Huntington Library has digitized the baptismal, marriage and burial records for the California Missions from 1769-1850. Through the Early California Population Project, I learned that Luz baptized her daughter, Manuela, on January 2, 1829,[147] and her other daughter, Petra, on July 6, 1832.[148] She gave birth to a son, José de la Cruz, who was baptized on June 3, 1836.[149] These were exciting discoveries since I had never seen any mention of these children in stories written about William. According to the Los Angeles Register of 1836, Luz Valencia was living in the Wolfskill household after January of 1836 so it is possible that William was José de la Cruz's father. José also could have been fathered by Francisco Araujo, the silversmith neighbor, who Luz married on July 1, 1836. Perhaps there is a descendant out there who can unlock this mystery.

---

110 Permission to William Wolfskill to trap beavers (nutria) on September 2, 1830, translated by J. Richard Salazar. Santa Fe Archives, Governor's Letterbook of Communications to officials in New Mexico, Roll 10, Frame # 851-52.

111 Petition to become a Mexican Citizen by José Guillermo Wolfskill, translated by J. Richard Salazar, Mexican Archives of New Mexico, Microfilm Reel #11, frames 213-217, Records of the *Ayuntamiento deTaos.*

112 Ibid.

113 Ibid.

114 Higbie Wilson, *William Wolfskill: 1798-1866 Frontier Trapper to California Ranchero,* 83.

115 J.M. Guinn, *A History of California and An Extended History of Los Angeles and Environs* (Los Angeles: Historic Record Company, 1915), Volume 1, 81.

116 Higbie Wilson, *William Wolfskill: 1798-1866 Frontier Trapper to California Ranchero,* 84.

117 Ibid., 85.

118 Manuela Valencia was born in 1829, *The Huntington Library, Early California Population Project Database, 2006,* baptismal record LA 00147. Manuela's sister, Petra Valencia, was born in July of 1832 and died in July, 1833. *The Huntington Library, Early California Population Project Database, 2006,* baptismal record SG 07793 and burial record LA 00183. María de la Luz Valencia, William's common-law wife, was also known as Luz Valencia.

119 *The Huntington Library, Early California Population Project Database, 2006,* baptismal record LA 00398.

120 Ibid., baptismal record LA 00489.

121 Los Angeles City Archive, January 14, 1836 session of the *ayuntamiento.*

122 Los Angeles City Archive, "Register of Los Angeles and its Jurisdiction: Year 1836," 465-466.

123 María Raquél Casas, *Married to a Daughter of the Land: Spanish-Mexican Women and Interethnic Marriage in California, 1820-1880* (Reno and Las Vegas: University of Nevada Press, 2007), 130.

124 Fremont Older, *California Missions and their Romances* (New York: Tudor Publishing Co., 1945), 67-68.

125 Casas, *Married to a Daughter of the Land: Spanish-Mexican Women and Interethnic Marriage in California, 1820-1880,* 130.

126 Los Angeles City Archives, Box B-1366, Minute Book of the City Council of the City of Los Angeles, April 7, 1836, Extraordinary Sessions, 136-138.

127 Los Angeles City Archives, Vigilante Execution of Gervacio Alipáz and María del Rosario Villa. William Wolfskill was listed as Guillermo Wolfskill in the Petition to the City Council, 138-139.

128   Ibid., 136-138.

129   Ibid., 138.

130   Ibid., 140.

131   Victoriano Vega, *Vida Californiana 1834-1847*, (Bancroft Library: 1877), 17.

132   Older, *California Missions and their Romances*, 68.

133   Los Angeles City Archives, Box B- 1366, 141.

134   Guinn, *A History of California and An Extended History of Los Angeles and Environs*, 102.

135   Manuela was listed as "Man'la Valencia Wolfskill" and 6 years old in the 1836 Register. But then she disappeared from any further mention in the Wolfskill family story so it appears that Luz took Manuela with her when she left William Wolfskill in 1836. Manuela resurfaced many years later.

136   The 1836 Los Angeles Register shows William Wolfskill, Luz Valencia, Susana, Timoteo and Manuela all living together in the same household. However, José de la Cruz's baptismal record from June 3, 1836 shows his father as "Unknown" or "No conoci-do" and gives his last name as Valencia. In other words, William Wolfskill is not acknowledged as the father. This leads me to think that Luz must have left William Wolfskill sometime before José de la Cruz's baptism in June. I don't think that she would have put the father as "Unknown" on the baptismal record if she had still been living with William. *The Huntington Library, Early California Population Project Database, 2006*, baptismal record LA 00607.

137   Marriage Register for San Gabriel Mission 1774-1855, Santa Barbara Mission Archive-Library.

138   *The Huntington Library, Early California Population Project Database, 2006*, baptismal record LA 00607.

139   Vega, *Vida Californiana 1834-1847*, 18.

140   William David Estrada, *The Los Angeles Plaza: Sacred and Contested Space* (Austin: University of Texas Press, 2008), 32-33.

141   A Mestizo is a person of mixed race of Native American and European ancestry in Mexico and Latin America.

142   A Mulatto is a person of mixed race of Black and Caucasian ancestry.

143   William M. Mason, *Los Angeles Under the Spanish Flag: Spain's New World* (Burbank: Southern California Genealogical Society, Inc., 2004), 66.

144   William David Estrada, *The Los Angeles Plaza: Sacred and Contested Space*, 31.

145   Mason, *Los Angeles Under the Spanish Flag: Spain's New World*, 66.

146   John Albert Wilson, *Thompson and West's History of Los Angeles County* (Oakland: 1880. Reproduction, Berkeley, California: Howell-North, 1959), 26.

147   *The Huntington Library, Early California Population Project Database, 2006*, baptismal record LA 00147.

148   *Ibid.*, baptismal record SG 07793.

149   *Ibid.*, baptismal record LA 00607.

CHAPTER 8

JOHN REID WOLFSKILL COMES TO CALIFORNIA

William's Story

William missed his family in Missouri but was so busy that he could not take the months off to travel back to Boone's Lick. On February 14, 1838, when William was away in the mountains, John Reid Wolfskill, his younger brother, arrived in Los Angeles on the back of a mule after a long and difficult journey over the Old Spanish Trail. The weather had been some of the coldest John Reid had ever experienced, and he was happy to be in the warmer *El Pueblo de Los Angeles* climate.

As John Reid rode down Main Street, he saw a very tall man, standing in the doorway of a store. Thinking he looked friendly, John Reid stopped and inquired if he might know where Billy Wolfskill could be found.[150]

"That rascal," chuckled the man, "Why he's up in the mountains getting some wood to build his wine barrels." Extending his hand in greeting, he continued,

"I'm John Warner, also known as Juan José Warner in these parts though some people call me Long John and some call me Don Juan Largo.[151] And who are you, if I might ask?" He wondered who this gaunt stranger could be.

"I'm John Reid Wolfskill. Just arrived from Santa Fe and hopin' to find my brother, Billy. Can you help me?"

"Why sure I can. Tie up your mule and come on inside. Let's get you some food."

Six foot three and born in Lyme, Connecticut,[152] Jonathan Trumbull Warner, also known as Juan José Warner, had a shop on Main Street in the pueblo. The news spread through town that William Wolfskill's brother was at Warner's store and was hoping to find him. One of William's good friends, Don Antonio María Lugo, arrived on horseback and offered to ride out to the mountains to notify William.[153]

William was engrossed in cutting wood for his wine barrels when Don Antonio rode up with the news of his brother's arrival at the pueblo. In his haste, Don Antonio had forgotten to ask his brother's name, so as William hurried to town, he had no idea which of his many brothers had arrived. When he reached Warner's shop, he saw a thin man waiting for him.

"Hello, brother," said William in a hesitating voice, confused by the man before him. Could this be John Reid he wondered but he was too thin, too weather beaten. Perhaps it was one of his other brothers—Mathus or Sarchel.

"Don't you know who I am? Billy, I'm your brother...John Reid. Well I guess I've changed a lot. Life has been pretty hard. I got really sick in Durango. Bandits stole all my mules from me last year in Mexico. I nearly lost everythin'. They even took most of my clothes."[154] He took a deep breath and continued.

"I want to make a fresh start. I'm willin' to help you with whatever you need."

William gave his brother a hug, overjoyed at having him in Los Angeles but concerned at seeing him so changed.

"Brother, you're always welcome." William put his arm around his brother's bony shoulders. All the hardship John Reid had suffered in Mexico and on the trail from Santa Fe showed on his brother's thin face.

"But you need something to eat. Why, we've got to fatten you up. And I want to hear how the family is."

John Reid jumped into working with his brother right away. As William spent more time tending to his small patch of grape vines on High Street, he realized how much he loved working on the land which led him in 1838 to acquire a plot of about one hundred acres that stretched from present-day Alameda to San Pedro and Third Street to Ninth Street. Moving to a larger piece of land gave William the space he needed to start his orchards and vineyards on a large scale. William was now on the outskirts of the pueblo, which suited him just fine since he could stay out of its shifting political turbulences. Excited about having more land, he planted his vineyard declaring that the vines, "well cared for, will last a hundred years."[155] With his brother, John Reid, helping him, William continued to plant many new vines.

Following the custom of the times, William built a large rectangular one-story adobe with walls made from mud and straw that were three to four feet thick and kept the temperature inside cool in the summer and warm in the winter. Known as the "Old Adobe," and the "Wolfskill Adobe," its many rooms opened onto the wide veranda that ran around the outside of the adobe where William would sit in the evening.

Wolfskill "Old Adobe"
Courtesy of Elena Wolfskill Thornton

Meanwhile the pueblo was buffeted by opposing political factions that pitted people in the north especially around Monterey against those in the south. People in the northern part of Alta California were loyal to Governor Alvarado while another group, including many of William's friends, supported Carlos Antonio Carrillo who had been appointed governor in 1837. In April of 1838, the residents of the pueblo awakened to see a large group of soldiers camped out on the plaza. Their commander, Clemente Espinosa, had been sent by a supporter of Governor Alvarado to arrest some of the most respected citizens of the pueblo including William's friends, Pío Pico and his brother Andrés, who were allies of Carlos Antonio Carrillo.[156]

Juan José Warner and his wife were having breakfast at their shop when a loud knocking at their door interrupted the morning calm.

"We are looking for Pío Pico. We need to search your house," stated several soldiers fingering their rifles.

"I assure you that Don Pico is not here," said Warner who had cracked the door open and started to shut it.

"I order you to let us in! We need to see for ourselves if he is hiding in your house," said the soldier in an impatient and stern voice.

The soldiers pushed the door open while Warner tried to prevent them from entering his house. Angry at being resisted, the soldiers attempted to arrest Warner who ran out into the street to avoid being taken prisoner. In an instant, Commander Espinosa appeared on the scene, and pointed his gun, ready to shoot. Warner, in self-defense, broke away from the soldier, lunged at Espinosa and knocked the gun from his hand. When he heard the shouting nearby, William Wolfskill grabbed his rifle and ran to investigate the trouble. Seeing that his good friend was in danger, he started to raise his rifle. Warner wanted to avoid bloodshed and quickly shouted,

"Don't shoot; I don't want any man killed."[157]

His plea for peace stopped the struggle, but William stood his ground with his rifle ready by his side. William was not a political man, but he was a loyal friend who would never tolerate injustice. He stayed by Warner who limped back to his store, holding his arm that had been broken in the fight. William kept a close eye on Commander Espinosa and was careful not to turn his back on him. William knew one false move could set off the commander and his soldiers.

"We're almost to the door, Long John."

As the two men reached the safety of Warner's shop, they opened the door and quickly went inside. The crisis had passed but William knew that it might only be a temporary pause in the storm.

~

PERSONAL OBSERVATIONS AND RESEARCH

Throughout my research on William Wolfskill, I am struck by his constant loyalty to his family. He had twelve siblings, four sisters, and eight brothers, including a set of twins. His mother, Sarah Reid Wolfskill, had a child almost every other year starting with William in 1798 in Kentucky and ending with Milton, who was born in Missouri in 1819.[158] Information on Sarah Reid Wolfskill stops after Milton's birth, and I have not been able to find the date of her death. Therefore, I have not included her in the book in events that happened after 1819. We do know that William's father, Joseph Wolfskill, lived in Missouri until his death in 1839.

William kept a close relationship with his brother, John Reid Wolfskill, who was born in Kentucky in 1804 and lived on William's farm in *El Pueblo de Los Angeles* from 1838 until 1842 helping to build up the Wolfskill vineyards and orchards. Together they planted the first orange grove on the new farm in 1841.

John Reid Wolfskill
Courtesy of UC Irvine Libraries, Special Collections
and Archives, Pleasants Family Papers

William also had great loyalty to his friends. He gave a helping hand to those who were close to him like his good friend, Jonathan Trumbull Warner, born in Connecticut, who traveled from Missouri to Santa Fe on a trading expedition. Later, Warner traveled to

California where he settled down and became a Mexican citizen, calling himself Juan José Warner.[159]

This chapter shows William's loyalty to his brother, John Reid, who was invited to live with William after John Reid had suffered many financial setbacks during his trading expeditions in Mexico. William's loyalty to Juan José Warner was evident when William refused to back down when he and Warner were faced with hostile Mexican forces at gun point.

150 H.D. Barrows, "A Pioneer of Sacramento Valley," *Publications of the Historical Society of Southern California* (Volume IV, Read March, 1895): 12-17.

151 The word "Don" was a title placed before the name of a man in Spanish-speaking Alta California to indicate respect.

152 H.D. Barrows, "Memorial Sketch of Col. J.J. Warner," *Annual Publication of the Historical Society of Southern California, Los Angeles, 1895*, 23 and 27.

153 H.D. Barrows, "A Pioneer of Sacramento Valley," 13.

154 Ibid., 13.

155 Colonel J.J. Warner, Judge Benjamin Hayes, Dr. J.P. Widney, *An Historical Sketch of Los Angeles County* (Louis Lewin & CO., 1876. Reprint, Los Angeles, California: O.W. Smith, Publisher, 1936), 120.

156 Ibid., 26.

157 Emma Adams, *To and Fro in Southern California* (1887, Reprint. New York: Arno Press A New York Times Company, 1976) 157-159. Emma Adams quoted these words in her account of the confrontation between Juan José Warner and Commander Espinosa.

158 http://wc.rootsweb.ancestry.com/cgi-bin/igm.cgi?op=GET&db=milliken1&id =I16079 Accessed 12-1-16. The information was compiled by Michael Milliken who has done much research on the Wolfskill family.

159 H.D. Barrows, "Memorial Sketch of Col. J.J. Warner,"23.

CHAPTER 9

WILLIAM WOLFSKILL MARRIES
MAGDALENA LUGO

William's Story

William was often invited by Don Antonio María Lugo to his adobe for fiestas. Don Antonio was a colorful personality who frequently dressed in Spanish outfits from the early days and spoke only in his native Spanish language.[160] A respected horseman and honored to have been a soldier, he always had the demeanor of an ex-military man and could be seen riding horseback around the pueblo with an elaborate sword strapped to his silver-adorned saddle.[161] He was rewarded in 1810 for his excellent service in the Spanish military with the land grant *Rancho San Antonio*, consisting of about 29,500 acres covering present-day Lynwood, Bell, Montebello and Maywood.[162]

They had been friends ever since 1831 when William had stopped at Don Antonio's ranch penniless and exhausted after the long journey from New Mexico over the Old Spanish Trail. They reminisced about those early days when William arrived fresh off the trail with his group of trappers all needing a good meal and some fresh clothes. Don Antonio had provided warm *Californio* hospitality to William and the members of his expedition, which resulted in a life-long friendship between the two men. William always looked forward to seeing his old friend and sharing a glass of brandy or *aguardiente*.

On this particular night in 1840, Don Antonio welcomed William to his fiesta and then introduced him to his niece, Magdalena Lugo, who was visiting from Santa Barbara.[163] Magdalena was lovely and in her mid-thirties.

"Magdalena, this is my good friend, Guillermo Wolfskill. I've known him for years. He has many interesting stories to tell you about his time trapping around Santa Fe. I trust you will take good care of my niece, Guillermo."

Don Antonio smiled and then left the two to become acquainted. William felt drawn to this woman who was attractive but modest. Being a bit older, she was not flirtatious like other young women he had met in the pueblo. Reserved at first, she opened up and told him about her work with the Indians at the Santa Barbara Mission helping the Franciscan friars.[164] Her brown eyes sparkled when she related stories about the Indian children. As the evening wore on, William became more attracted to Magdalena and asked if he could visit with her again during her stay with Don Antonio. Magdalena blushed and nodded that she too would like to see him again.

Coming back to his adobe with its many empty rooms, William felt he was ready to enlarge his family. The memories of Luz had faded and now he longed for the companionship of a wife. William and Magdalena became friends, fell in love and were married at the Santa Barbara Presidio on January 12, 1841, by Franciscan Padre Narciso Durán.[165.] In the marriage book, Father Durán noted that "Guillermo Urquides, a single man," and "Magdalena Lugo, a single woman" were joined in matrimony. The Wolfskill name was difficult to pronounce so William was known by a number of names including Guillermo Urquides.

Marriage Entry for Guillermo Urquides and Magdalena Lugo 1841
Courtesy of the Santa Bárbara Mission Archive-Library

Magdalena and William returned to Los Angeles from Santa Barbara on board the ship *Bolivar* on Sunday, January 17, 1841.[166] They stood on the deck waving to her family and friends as the crowds and the town of Santa Barbara became smaller and smaller on the horizon. Buffeted by the cold winter wind, Magdalena drew her wool cloak closer around her. She and William waited until the last speck of Santa Barbara had disappeared.

"*Mi querida* Magdalena," whispered William as he put his arm around her and gave her a kiss. "Shall we go inside where it's warmer?"

"*Si, mi amor*," she replied. "I know I will miss my family and my friends. It's hard to say goodbye. But we are a family now. I'm looking forward to seeing Susana and Timoteo. I miss them."

"Magdalena, it's so wonderful to have you by my side. I have many plans for our family and our farm." The love William experienced for Magdalena was unlike any he had felt before. His deep intuition told him she would be a special wife as well as a loving mother.

The year 1841 was a good year for William and his new bride. Planting about 60 to 80 orange trees near his adobe home, William started an orchard on two acres that would eventually grow into one of the premiere orange groves in Los Angeles and the United States.[167] The orange trees came from the fertile gardens of the San Gabriel Mission, which Father Sánchez had shown William when he had first arrived in Los Angeles 10 years earlier.

Later that year, happiness arrived at the "Old Adobe" in the form of William and Magdalena's first child, a little daughter, named Juana Josefa, also known as Juanita, who was baptized at the plaza church on November 23. María de las Nieves Guirado, a friend of the Wolfskill family, was Juana's *madrina* or godparent[168] and later became *madrina* to all of Magdalena and William's children. William often told people that his first orange grove dated from 1841 when Juana was born.[169]

While his family life was prospering, William's relationship with his brother, John Reid, was becoming tense since John seemed restless and somewhat irritable these days. When John first arrived, things were harmonious with both brothers working hard at planting vines on William's new property. But in 1840, John had traveled to Northern California hoping to find his own land. On the advice of Juan José Warner, John Reid had traveled northeasterly towards Sutter's Fort where he found an area near present-day Winters, California, that had a creek and some high ground[170] where he could build a house, plant crops and graze cattle. Covered by acres of wild oats that grew as tall as the backside of a horse,[171] this land had everything that John Reid could ask for—water, fertile soil, and good drainage. Only one thing was missing. General Mariano Guadalupe Vallejo, the commanding officer in Sonoma, had rebuffed John Reid's request for a land grant because he was not a Mexican citizen.

Tall, good-looking, with intense dark eyes and a wide forehead, *Comandante* Mariano Vallejo was an imposing figure and highly educated.[172] His father, Don Ignacio Vallejo, had been part of the military guard that accompanied Father Junipero Serra in the early establishment of the missions in California.[173] A proud military man, Mariano Vallejo ruled with an iron fist. He had been named Military Commander and Director of Colonization of the Northern Frontier by Governor José Figueroa.[174] Vallejo took his position as *comandante* or commander seriously. He supported bringing Mexican settlers and families to the Sonoma area in order to solidify Mexican governance of the northern frontier, but he was not encouraging to foreigners like John Reid Wolfskill.

Undaunted by Vallejo's rejection, John Reid traveled back to Sonoma in 1841. William waited impatiently in the pueblo for John to return and share the results of this last trip to Northern California. At last, John Reid arrived at the adobe tired from the long journey from Sonoma. His voice cracked from exhaustion but his dark eyes sparkled with excitement as he recounted his recent conversation with General Mariano Vallejo whose decision determined the next stage of John Reid's life.

"Brother, the trip was hard. I was very discouraged since Vallejo was opposed to grantin' me any land. But Jacob Leese offered to talk to the *comandante*. I had actually lost all hope. Then Jacob announced that Vallejo would no longer stand in my way. But there is one catch. Billy, since you are a Mexican citizen, you must ask for the land. He will still not grant it to me because I am an American citizen."

William listened. Jacob Leese was a friendly man married to General Vallejo's sister. Born in Ohio but now a Mexican citizen, he was close to Vallejo. Leese had done a good job of persuading the *comandante*. Besides, Magdalena's aunt, María Antonia Lugo de Vallejo, was the *comandante's* mother so perhaps he felt some familial loyalty to Magdalena.[175]

"And the best news of all, Vallejo has agreed that you can have four square leagues on the banks of Putah Creek.[176] Now you need to make a formal request." John Reid's look became intense as he waited for his brother's reply.

"Are you sure you want to settle there so far away from the pueblo and your family?" William asked, hoping that his brother might change his mind. William wanted to help his younger brother but felt deep regret at the thought of John Reid moving to the north.

"Billy, now that you're married, you'll be spendin' time with Magdalena... havin' more children. Soon I'll be in your way. It's time for me to have my own farm and my own life."

"Let me think about this. It's so far away and we'll hardly get to see you. Are you sure?" But William knew his brother would leave and he felt great sadness. He was the link that helped him stay connected to his family.

Meanwhile, William spent his days planting more grape vines and orange trees. He was sad to see his brother leave for the north in 1842, but he knew that John Reid needed to strike out on his own. William asked General Mariano Vallejo for the land in Northern California that his brother wanted so badly. Vallejo finally gave his approval for approximately 17,700 acres, however, they were still waiting for the land grant, called *Rancho Río de los Putos*, to be authorized and signed by Governor Juan Bautista de Alvarado. These matters could drag on when dealing with governmental officials in the north in Sonoma and Monterey, far from the pueblo.

William watched as John Reid took one last look at the vineyards and orchards he had helped to plant over the past four years since his arrival at William's farm.

"Take this with you. It will protect you," smiled Magdalena as she placed a small crucifix in John's hand. "My father gave this to me, and I now pass this along to you. *Buena suerte* in your new home. I wish you all the good luck in the world."

"*Tío Juan*, Mama, Papa and I will come and visit you someday," said Susana now eight as she gave a last hug to her uncle. "I wish you were not goin'."

"And I'll come and see you too," added Timoteo who did not want to be ignored.

"I'll be back," promised John Reid. "Maybe next spring."

"Brother, if you have any problems, you can stay with George Yount. He'll probably have some work for you too. Have a safe journey and may God bless you."

William watched his brother head out on the next chapter of his life, driving a small herd of cattle, oxen and horses. It was a bittersweet moment with William filled with both unhappiness and anticipation of the new things to come for his brother.

~9

Personal Observations and Research

Unfortunately, there is not extensive information about Magdalena Lugo, who married William in 1841, or Luz Valencia, his common-law wife with whom he lived in the early to mid-1830s. We know more about Magdalena Lugo who was descended from the Lugos and Romeros, both prominent *Californio* families of Santa Barbara. Her grandfather, Francisco Salvador Lugo, had been part of the military guard during the founding and early days of *El Pueblo de Los Angeles* as well as having served in different military posts, eventually settling in Santa Barbara.

José Ygnacio Lugo, Francisco Salvador's son and Magdalena's father, was also a career soldier and a *"soldado de cuera"* or "leather jacket" soldier.[177] The *soldados de cuera* belonged to a specialized group of soldiers, who defended the presidios and missions in Alta California under Spanish rule and were recognizable due to their thick leather jackets that protected them during fighting.

Born in May of 1804, Magdalena Lugo grew up in Santa Barbara where she spent time during her youth working with the Franciscan friars. According to historian, Iris Higbie Wilson, Magdalena, as a young woman, helped teach the Indians at the Santa Barbara Mission.[178] After meeting William during a visit with her uncle, Don Antonio María Lugo, who lived in the pueblo, Magdalena and William fell in love and were married.

Since we have never heard of a previous marriage for Magdalena, she must have been considered somewhat "old" at 36 because most women married at a young age during those times. Her work with the friars could explain why she didn't marry until later in life. After their marriage, William and Magdalena sold oranges from the four trees in front of the adobe and donated the proceeds to the Santa Barbara Mission.[179] I remember my mother mentioning when I was growing up that she had heard from the older Wolfskills that the Indians who needed food were never turned away from the "Old Adobe."

I have searched for but never found a photograph or painting of Magdalena. Henri Penelon, outstanding artist of the pueblo, painted and took photos of the leading citizens of Los Angeles during the 1860s but did not record Magdalena's image. I imagine that she was beautiful since we have photos of her six children and they are all attractive with dark hair and brown eyes, reflecting their Spanish and Mexican heritages.

---

160 H.D. Barrows, "Don Antonio María Lugo: A Picturesque Character of California," *Annual Publication of the Historical Society of Southern California, Los Angeles, Volume 3, No. 4 (1896)*: 28-34.

161 Harris Newmark, *Sixty Years in Southern California: 1853-1913*, eds. Maurice H. and Marco R. Newmark (Los Angeles, 1916; Los Angeles: Dawson's Book Shop, 1984), 263. Newmark was a successful merchant who also was interested in history. His book is an important source of early Los Angeles history.

162 Robert G. Cowan, *Ranchos of California: A List of Spanish Concessions 1775-1822 and Mexican Grants 1822-1846* (Fresno, California: Academy Library Guild, 1956), 71-72.

163 Higbie Wilson, *William Wolfskill: 1798-1866 Frontier Trapper to California Ranchero*, 107. This scene is based on Magdalena's visit to her uncle's home in the pueblo where she first met William.

164 Higbie Wilson, *William Wolfskill: 1798-1866 Frontier Trapper to California Ranchero*, 109. Higbie Wilson mentions in her book that Magdalena helped the friars at the Santa Barbara Mission teach the Indians which I have included in this scene.

165 Marriage book from the Santa Barbara Mission, "Año 1841" (translated "Year 1841") item 233.

166 Higbie Wilson, *William Wolfskill: 1798-1866 Frontier Trapper to California Ranchero*, 107.

167 Albert Wilson, *Thompson and West's History of Los Angeles County*, 183.

168 *The Huntington Library, Early California Population Project, 2006*, baptismal record LA 01099.

169 Colonel J.J. Warner, Judge Benjamin Hayes, Dr. J.P. Widney, *An Historical Sketch of Los Angeles County*, 120.

170 "Winters Express" Reprint from the 1975 Centennial Edition of the Winters Express. The article consists of excerpts from "John Reid Wolfskill, the Pioneer of Solano County" by Brooks C. Sackett.

171 Ned Wolfskill, *A Few of the Things I Remember as Told Me by My Father, the Late J.R. Wolfskill*, 9.

172 Myrtle M. McKittrick, *Vallejo: Son of California* (Portland, Oregon: Binfords & Mort, Publishers, 1944), 292.

173 Ibid,1.

174 Ibid., 71.

175 María Antonia Lugo married Ignacio Vallejo and was Mariano Vallejo's mother. She was the daughter of Francisco Salvador Lugo and is my great-great-great-aunt (third great-aunt).

176 Barrows, "A Pioneer of Sacramento Valley," 14. Four Leagues would be about 17,700 acres.

177 *The Huntington Library, Early California Population Project Database, 2006*, marriage record BP 00043. It was stated in the marriage record that José was a soldado de cuera.

178 Higbie Wilson, *William Wolfskill: 1798-1866 Frontier Trapper to California Ranchero*, 109.

179 Ibid.

CHAPTER 10

THE WOLFSKILL BROTHERS ESTABLISH RANCHO RÍO DE LOS PUTOS

William's Story

The final approval for William's land grant in Northern California was a challenge given the distance between the *El Pueblo de Los Angeles* and Sonoma where *Comandante* Mariano Vallejo was headquartered. On February 6, 1842, William petitioned Vallejo, requesting the *Rancho Río de los Putos* land:

> I, William Wolfskill, a resident of this National Department of the Upper California before your honor respectfully show that possessing a certain quantity of large and small cattle and not having any place wherein to put them unless your honor may please to grant to me a tract of land ... called *Río de los Putos* situated on the north of this frontier...and to grant to me the aforesaid land. I ask that it consist of four square leagues...[180]

After many delays, General Vallejo gave his approval once he had seen William's Mexican citizenship papers. The land grant for *Rancho Río de los Putos* was issued on May 24, 1842, by California Governor Juan

Bautista de Alvarado to William Wolfskill, a Mexican citizen in the following document:

> Whereas, William Wolfskill, a naturalized Mexican, for his benefit and that of his family, has made application for a tract of land bounded on the East by the Bullrush Swamp and on the West by the hills and located on the banks of the River called *Los Putos*, having previously taken the legal steps and made the proper investigations agreeable to the provisions of the laws and regulations, by virtue of the powers conferred upon me in the name of the Mexican Nations, I have granted him the above mentioned land declaring him the owner of it by these letters...[181]

Rancho Río de Los Putos Land Grant Map E-508
Courtesy of the Bancroft Library, University of California, Berkeley

William had heard from John Reid that as anxious as he was to get to *Rancho Río de los Putos*, he was staying with George Yount, William's fellow trapper from the Old Spanish Trail, until he could take his herd across the San Joaquin River, which was impassable due to flooding. John had left his animals near the Dolores Mission about a mile from Yerba Buena. At that time, Yerba Buena, which would eventually grow into the city of San Francisco, was a small town of only 50 residents.[182] John reported that he was helping George build a mill on Napa Creek.

After arriving in California with William in 1831 from their journey on the Old Spanish Trail, George Yount had traveled north and settled in present-day Napa Valley in 1836 on a land grant consisting of about 12,000 acres called *Rancho Caymus*.[183] Living alone on his large ranch, George built both a log blockhouse and adobe fort to serve as protection from hostile attacks.[184] Though William knew that John Reid was in good hands with his friend, George Yount, he still worried about his brother starting off a new farm without the right seeds and tools. On May 30, 1842, William sent corn, beans, shovels, spades and two barrels of brandy or a*guardiente* with various people traveling north and a letter to "Señor Juan Wolfskill Care of Mr. Yount":

Dear Brother

I sent your corn & beans by Mr. Thompson, 2 shovels & 1 spade by Mr. Wilson, two barrels of auguardiente & your blanket, 3 sheets & pillow & two cases by Mr. Hastings, your saddle bridle and 2 buckets...

...If you wish to trade with any of the ship owners sell them wine or auguardiente. I will deliver it as soon as it is made or

if you want any sent up let me know & it shall be sent immediately. Please write by the first opportunity & then every
other chance and you will very much oblige your brother,

William Wolfskill[185]

John spent the next several months with George Yount but grew
eager to start his own farm. He returned to Yerba Buena to pick up
his herd of cattle and headed towards Putah Creek where he arrived
in the summer of 1842.

Rancho Río de los Putos extended for miles and encompassed dense
wilderness of wild animals as well as fertile open pasture land and oak
groves. On his first day, John saw several grizzly bears and mountain
lions in the area so he spent the night high up in a tree safe from the
prowling animals. From his days on the frontier in Missouri, John
knew how critical a garden would be for his survival leading him to
immediately clear out brush and plant a vegetable garden with seeds
and cuttings that he had brought up from William's farm in the
pueblo.[186] He also built a hut made from tule reeds and mud where he
could live while he started up the *rancho*. This was important since
the first condition of obtaining the land grant stipulated that a house
needed to be erected and inhabited within a year—a requirement
that William and John Reid were able to satisfy.[187]

It was a lonely existence. An Indian trail crossed his land and
there were several Patwin Indian villages along Putah Creek. John
Reid would occasionally see his Patwin neighbors traveling up and
down the creek, but he once went five weeks without seeing another
human being.[188] Sometimes the only movement would be from a
mountain lion or grizzly bear, which forced John Reid to be vigilant
at all times. Slowly he laid claim to the land.

Meanwhile the political events of California were continuing to swirl in unending intrigue. In August of 1842, General Manuel Micheltorena arrived in California by order of the Mexican government to replace Governor Alvarado. Feted by the citizens of *El Pueblo de Los Angeles* with numerous balls, bullfights, fandangos and parties, Micheltorena stayed in the south instead of traveling to Monterey in the north, which served as the capitol of Alta California.[189] Within a short time, Micheltorena grew unpopular due to his army composed of many ex-convicts from Mexican prisons who mistreated the residents. Hungry and poorly paid, the soldiers raided the chicken coops, vineyards, orchards and vegetable gardens throughout the pueblo leaving a swath of bad will.[190] As his army "devoured the country like an army of *chapules* [locusts],"[191] Micheltorena remained in Los Angeles for several months before moving on to Monterey to become the official governor.

On October 19, 1842, the commander of the United States Pacific Squadron, Commodore Thomas ap Catesby Jones, sailed into Monterey harbor on hearing a rumor that the United States and Mexico were at war. He demanded that Monterey surrender to the American forces replacing the Mexican flag with the American Stars and Stripes. However, when Jones received the news that the United States had not declared war with Mexico, he withdrew the American flag from Monterey, returned the Mexican flag to its rightful place and traveled south to personally apologize to Micheltorena for his mistake.[192]

With so many conflicting factions, William felt it best to stay away from political activity. Instead, he concentrated on helping his brother with the new *rancho*. On January 15, 1843, William sent him 1200 vines and boxes of fruit trees, potatoes, seeds and beans, writing in his letter:

Dear Brother

...I could not find any corn and the wine you sent for is not fit for shipping yet though I will send it as soon as I can...If you have had a chance to find a good vine of our Missouri river grapes, I wish you would send me ½ dozen of slips. Be sure to write me by the first opportunity if you have received the one hundred head of cattle...

Your affectionate brother
William Wolfskill[193]

Throughout that year, William continued to send him more cattle, barrels of wine, saddles and saddle blankets.

On June 10, 1843, William asked his brother if he wanted more land:

Dear Brother

...If you wish to have more added to your *Rancho* you can have it or if you wish to have another it can be obtained from the present governor as he is more disposed to give lands to foreigners than to let them lay idle...[194]

When John was not quick in replying to his letters, William wrote his brother on August 7, 1843, that he "was disappointed in not receiving a letter from you ..." and later in the letter asked him to "give me a full discription of the country & people & everything worth my hearing, your affectionate brother William Wolfskill."[195]

While William was very busy helping his brother establish *Rancho Río de los Putos*, Magdalena gave birth to another daughter,

Francisca Wolfskill, baptized on June 13, 1843, at the little church on the plaza also known as *La Placita* Church.[196]

Meanwhile, William and his brother found themselves in a land dispute with their neighbors. Juan Manuel Vaca and Juan Felipe Peña were New Mexicans who had traveled over the Old Spanish Trail with the Workman-Rowland expedition in 1841. On June 6, 1842, Juan Manuel Vaca petitioned for a land grant called *Rancho Lihuaytos* which was adjacent to the Wolfskill *Rancho*.[197] *Rancho Lihuaytos* was granted on January 27, 1843 as 10 leagues.[198] However, the boundaries actually stretched over almost twice that area and overlapped with part of the Wolfskills' *Rancho Río de los Putos*.[199] Trouble began when Vaca's cattle started roaming onto the Wolfskill land looking for water. With both parties claiming some of the same land, Vallejo ordered John Reid Wolfskill to leave.[200]

When John Reid turned to Jacob Leese, Vallejo's brother-in-law, for help he was told that he would have to obey *Comandante* Vallejo's orders. In June of 1844, Governor Micheltorena issued additional orders requiring the Wolfskills to leave their land.[201] John Reid knew he had few rights since he was not a Mexican citizen. With William so far away in the pueblo and unable to help, John moved his cattle to the Gordon Ranch at Cache Creek and waited for the opportunity to fight back.[202]

At the same time, the political situation throughout Alta California was becoming more unstable. People were upset with Governor Micheltorena and his band of convicts but so far had not fought against his unfair governance. However, resentment was growing and the Wolfskills hoped the time would soon come to settle their boundary dispute and regain their land.

Careful to stay out of partisan politics, William signed on to serve as *regidor* or council member of *El Ayuntamiento* of Los Angeles in 1844 drawn by a sense of duty to his community.[203] All city councils or *ayuntamientos* in Alta California had been closed on January 1, 1840, because none of the towns had a large enough population to warrant having a city council under Mexican Law.[204] But in 1844, the *ayuntamientos* were re-established and with that a call to serve.

William was glad that the pueblo's city council had been reinstated so that now they could solve some of the problems facing the residents. He dressed in his best black suit as he prepared for his first meeting of the "Most Illustrious" City Council or *"Muy Illustre" Ayuntamiento*. He and his fellow council members would oversee the most important issues of the community in addition to some of the smaller needs such as straightening fences. The *ayuntamiento* had authority over an area as large as the State of Massachusetts. There was much work and no pay.[205]

"Ay, Guillermo, you are *muy guapo* today —very handsome. May you be filled with patience and understanding on your first day with the *ayuntamiento*." Magdalena was so proud of her husband.

"*Mi querida*, it's my duty. I'm certainly not doing this for the money. I've heard that the mayor is going to propose that a school be started for the young children of the pueblo."

Magdalena clapped her hands and exclaimed, "How wonderful. They need to learn how to read and write."

"Yes, and we must find a good teacher for the children," stated William. "Hopefully, there will be enough money to pay someone."

William then kissed his wife goodbye. "And hopefully, we won't have too many disputes right away."

At the January 5, 1844, city council meeting, Mayor Manuel Requena asked William, referred to as Guillermo Guisquiel on the council, to be on the water and police commissions along with his good friend Juan Bandini.[206] At the next session, the police commission set out a lengthy Code of Laws including the following regulations:

The normal penalties would be levied for such infractions as "the loss of hogs if kept loose in the town" or "running horses within the city limits." Saloonkeepers were warned to close by 8 PM or face fines. And homeowners were admonished to clean the front of their houses at least every Saturday and told that wagons should not be parked on the streets "where people pass" or a fine of "four bits" would be imposed for each offense.[207]

William attended the city council meetings throughout 1844 and helped decide land disputes and fence straightening questions as well as find funding for the new primary school teacher.

On September 15, 1844, Magdalena and William welcomed the birth of their first son, José Guillermo, baptized like his two sisters at the little church on the plaza.[208]

The year 1845 brought more political unrest as some of the most respected California citizens organized against Governor Micheltorena and his unruly army who continued to steal whatever they wanted from regular citizens. The revolutionists under the leadership of José Antonio Castro, the Pico brothers, and American supporters fought against the forces of Micheltorena in the Cahuenga Valley north of the pueblo on February 20, 1845. Taking advantage of a break in the fighting, Benjamin Wilson, William Workman and James McKinley, the Americans in Castro's army, climbed up a ravine and found the foreigners who backed Micheltorena.[209] They convinced them to stop their support of Micheltorena by promising that their lands would be safer under Pío Pico. When the foreigners abandoned Micheltorena, the battle ended without human bloodshed with the only victim being a mustang or a mule.[210] Micheltorena eventually left the United States for Mexico and Pío Pico became governor of California in 1845.[211]

Concerned that his brother's health was not good, William hoped that John might return to the pueblo and wrote on March 1, 1845:

Dear Brother

I am quite sorry to hear of your being so unwell. I should like if you could sell your cattle and come down here to live….

William then commented on the political unrest in California and wrote:

I am quite happy to think that you had the good judgment not to join in the revolution. We have Don Pío Pico for Governor and Don Juan Bandini Secretary of State. I have no more to say but remain your affectionate Brother.

William Wolfskill[212]

Meanwhile the land dispute between William Wolfskill and his neighbors, Vaca and Peña, escalated in July of 1845 ending up in the Primary Court of Claims in Los Angeles where, in a temporary agreement, Vaca was ordered to leave the Wolfskill land.[213] When the dispute flared up again, the court ordered that "Wolfskill should remain with the lands that he claimed on the upper part of the creek, and Vaca and Peña should take theirs adjoining his on the east."[214] After the land conflict was settled, Vaca petitioned for a new land grant.[215] Governor Pico subsequently issued a correcting grant to Juan Manuel Vaca and Juan Felipe Armijo (the latter also known as Peña) called *Rancho Los Putos* and ordered that the contested land must be returned to Wolfskill.[216] Practically speaking,

William regained possession of his land, but he would have to wait until 1854 to have the *rancho* confirmed by the United States Land Commission in the Wolfskill name.

~

PERSONAL OBSERVATIONS AND RESEARCH

In 2011, Rich and I visited Winters, California, to see what re-mained of William Wolfskill's land grant, *Rancho Río de los Putos*. Originally about 17, 700 acres of fertile land, the *rancho* stretched on the banks of Putah Creek.[217] We were intrigued by the name since in Spanish the word *"puta"* means "whore" leading us to wonder why the word would be used. There has been discussion about whether the word *"putos"* was used as an insult or because it sounded very similar to the Patwin word "Puttoy" used by the local Patwin Indians to describe themselves.[218] It could also have been influenced by the name of the indigenous Patwin village along the creek called "Putato" (or Poo-tah-toi).[219] I would like to think that *"los putos"* was chosen because it sounded similar to the Patwin words.

When I learned from a cousin that John Reid Wolfskill's daughter, Frances Wolfskill Taylor Wilson, donated 107 acres to the University of California, Davis in 1934 to be used as a farm,[220] I made an appointment to visit the Wolfskill Experimental Farm, also known as the Wolfskill Experimental Orchards, located on the outskirts of the small city of Winters, California. Rich and I stopped at the gate where a bronze plaque announced that we had reached the Wolfskill Experimental Farm, California Registered Historical Landmark Number 804. On the plaque was a brief description of John Reid's historical importance as "The Father of the Fruit Industry in the Region." The entrance to the farm was magnificent with the original olive trees planted in 1861 on both sides of the long driveway that led into the property.[221] One of Taylor's stipulations in giving the property to UC Davis was that these beautiful olive trees must be preserved "as a memorial to her parents and as a symbol of peace for the great State of California."[222]

California Historical Landmark 804
Wolfskill Experimental Farm in Winters, California
Photo by Richard Marusich

Entrance to Wolfskill Experimental Farm in Winters, California
Photo by Conchita Thornton Marusich

Tony Cristler, the Assistant Agricultural Superintendent of the Wolfskill Experimental Orchards, took us on a tour and showed us the date palm trees planted by John Reid Wolfskill that still stand tall and graceful. We next stopped at an orange tree with an old gnarled trunk planted from seeds long ago that may have come from William Wolfskill's orchards in the pueblo. William had sent many seeds and seedlings up to John Reid while he was establishing his *rancho*. Unfortunately, none of William's orchards still exist in Los Angeles, so it was a thrill to taste the sweet oranges we picked from the old, venerable tree that might have originated from William's farm. If only that orange tree could speak to us of its journey through the years.

Conchita and Rich Marusich in Front of
Old Wolfskill Orange Trees
Photo by Richard Marusich

The Wolfskill Experimental Farm is now an on-going witness
to the horticultural legacy of John Reid. Once the land was donated
to UC Davis, John Reid's dedication to agriculture has continued on
through research and development of new varieties of fruit including strawberries, peaches, cherries, almonds, prunes, and pistachios.
Plant breeding, environmental stress research and education are
other important agricultural activities at the farm. "Since 1980, The

Wolfskill Experimental Orchards have also been home to a USDA-run National Clonal Germplasm Repository, which keeps alive several hundred varieties of stone fruits, grapes, walnuts, pistachios, persimmons, olives, pomegranate, fig and kiwi."[223] As a Wolfskill, I am very proud to see how the land of our family continues to benefit the people of California and saddened at the same time that William's beautiful orchards have disappeared under concrete in Los Angeles.

As I researched the history of *Rancho Río de los Putos*, I learned about the land dispute that occurred between the Wolfskills and their neighbors, Juan Manuel Vaca and Juan Felipe Peña, the owners of the adjoining *Rancho Los Putos*. At that time, boundaries were often vaguely described which led to many misunderstandings and conflict. The old land grant *diseños* or maps are very simple, crude drawings that give general landmarks but lack specific measurements that characterize our maps today. In addition, landmarks such as streams can often change course and thereby affect boundaries.

I recently spoke with Cecelia Peña, great-great-granddaughter of Juan Felipe Peña, about her family's history and the land disagreement with the Wolfskills. She felt that the relationship between the Peñas and the Wolfskills had not suffered because of the land conflict. In fact, the Wolfskills were always seen as good neighbors.[224] Rich and I recently visited the Peña Adobe in Vacaville, California, where we saw the Valencia orange tree gifted by John Reid Wolfskill to the Peña family that still produces sweet oranges.

I sourced much information about John Reid Wolfskill and his descendants from the Wolfskill Family Collection that is part of the General Library's Special Collections Department at the University of California, Davis.[225] His son, Ned Wolfskill, wrote an unpublished manuscript entitled "A Few of the Things I Remember as

Told Me by My Father, the Late J.R. Wolfskill" containing wonderful anecdotes about John Reid that I had not read elsewhere and have included in my story. The Wolfskill Family Collection has many boxes of photos, letters, correspondence and documents that are an incredible resource for people wanting to learn more about this important pioneering family of Yolo and Solano Counties. It gave me a chance to increase my understanding about John Reid as well as my Wolfskill cousins from Northern California.

As I continued my research into William and John Reid's lives, I made an exciting discovery at the Huntington Library in San Marino in Southern California where I found a series of letters written by William to John Reid after his brother had moved to Northern California and started his farm at *Rancho Río de los Putos*. The letters are invaluable in expanding our understanding of William because they reveal much about his character as a caring brother and generous person who gave both financial support and encouragement to his brother's new venture in Northern California. In addition, the letters give great insight into the ups and downs of William's farming business, his concerns about his brother, the political upheavals occurring in California and his own future. Even though I could not find any letters from John Reid to William, we still glean a lot of information about both William and John Reid. From my research, these letters have not been cited in any other publication on William, which made their discovery even more thrilling.

William Wolfskill's Letter on May 30, 1842, to John Reid Wolfskill
Wolfskill Collection

Courtesy of the Huntington Library, San Marino, California

---

180 Land Grant *Rancho Río de los Putos*, Banc MSS land case files 232 Northern District (ND), Courtesy of the Bancroft Library, University of California, Berkeley, 64.
181 Land Grant *Rancho Río de los Putos*, Banc MSS land case files 232 Northern District (ND), Courtesy of the Bancroft Library, University of California, Berkeley, 66 and 67.

182   http://www.sfgenealogy.com/sf/history/hgpop.htm Yerba Buena, which later became San Francisco had a population of 50 people in 1844. Accessed on 12-1-16.

183   Cowan, *Ranchos of California: A List of Spanish Concessions 1775-1822 and Mexican Grants 1822-1846*, 25.

184   Camp, ed., *George C. Yount and his Chronicles of the West*, page xii.

185   Letter from William Wolfskill to John Reid Wolfskill, May 30, 1842, The Huntington Library, San Marino, California. The Wolfskill Collection.

186   Ned Wolfskill, *A Few of the Things I Remember as Told Me by My Father, the Late J.R. Wolfskill*, 10.

187   Land Grant *Rancho Río de los Putos*, Banc MSS land case files 232 Northern District (ND), 67.

188   Ned Wolfskill, *A Few of the Things I Remember as Told Me by My Father, the Late J.R. Wolfskill*, 10.

189   Albert Wilson, *Thompson and West's History of Los Angeles County*, 38.

190   Guinn, *A History of California and An Extended History of Los Angeles and Environs*, 110.

191   Ibid., 111.

192   Kevin Starr, *California: A History* (New York: The Modern Library, 2005) 60.

193   Letter to John Reid Wolfskill from William Wolfskill, January 15, 1843. The Huntington Library, San Marino, California. The Wolfskill Collection.

194   Ibid., June 10, 1843.

195   Ibid., August 7, 1843.

196   *The Huntington Library, Early California Population Project Database, 2006*, baptismal record LA 01208.

197   Expediente 424, *California Spanish Land Records 1784-1868*, Ancestry.com,[database on-line], Provo, UT, USA.

198   The United States v Juan Manuel Vaca and Juan Felipe Peña, http://openjurist. org/59/us/556/the-united-states-v-juan-manuel-vaca-and-juan-felipe-pena

199   Young Wood, *Vaca Peña Los Putos Rancho and the Peña Adobe*, (Vallejo: Wheeler Printing and Publishing:1965), 12.

200   Barrows, "A Pioneer of Sacramento Valley," 15-16.

201   Higbie Wilson, *William Wolfskill: 1798-1866 Frontier Trapper to California Ranchero*, 130.

202   Barrows, "A Pioneer of Sacramento Valley," 16.

203   Los Angeles Archives January 5, 1844 Minutes, Box 1366, 541.

204   Guinn, *A History of California and An Extended History of Los Angeles and Environs*. Guinn wrote: "In 1837 the Mexican Congress passed a degree abolishing *ayuntamientos* in capitals of departments having a population of less than four thousand and in interior towns of less than eight thousand." 114-115.

205   Ibid.

206   Los Angeles City Archives, January 5, 1844 Minutes, Box 1366, 541. Wolfskill was a difficult name in Spanish so William was often called Guillermo Guisquiel on the council and in the pueblo.

207   Ibid., 546-547.

208   *The Huntington Library, Early California Population Project Database, 2006*, baptismal record LA 01264.

209   Guinn, *A History of California and An Extended History of Los Angeles and Environs*, 112. Albert Wilson, *Thompson and West's History of Los Angeles County*, 41.

210   Ibid.

211   Albert Wilson, *Thompson and West's History of Los Angeles County*, 41.

212   Letter to John Reid Wolfskill from William Wolfskill, March 1, 1845, The Huntington Library, San Marino, California, The Wolfskill Collection.

213   Higbie Wilson, *William Wolfskill: 1798-1866 Frontier Trapper to California Ranchero*, 131.

214   The United States v Juan Manuel Vaca and Juan Felipe Peña.

215   Expediente 465, *California Spanish Land Records 1784-1868*, Ancestry.com, [database on-line], Provo, UT, USA.

216   The United States v Juan Manuel Vaca and Juan Felipe Peña.

217   Barrows, "A pioneer of Sacramento Valley", 14.

218   http://daviswiki.org/putah_creek. Accessed 12-1-16.

219   Erwin G. Gudde, *California Place Names: The Origen and Etymology of Current Geographical Names*, (University of California Press: 1965), 246.

220   Diane Nelson, "History Lessons," The Leaflet, UC Davis Plant Sciences, 20. http://ucanr.org/sites/wolfskill2/files/24267.pdf , 20.

221   Ibid., 19.

222   Based on an interview with Tony Cristler, Assistant Agricultural Superintendent of the Wolfskill Orchards, 2011.

223   Nelson, "History Lessons," The Leaflet, UC Davis Plant Sciences, 21.

224   Cecelia Peña., conversations on 1-10-2017 and 2-4-17.

225   UC Davis, General Library, Department of Special Collections, Wolfskill Family Collection.

CHAPTER 11

CALIFORNIA DESCENDS INTO WAR

William's Story

Life was good for Magdalena and William as they added another baby sister to the family. Little Magdalena, also called Madalena, was baptized at *La Placita* Church, on May 13, 1846, attended by her godparents María de las Nieves Guirado and her husband Alexander Bell.[226] Though Guirado and Bell had no children, according to Juan José Warner, "they were *Padrinos* [godfather and godmother] to more children than any other couple in California."[227]

The slow-paced rhythm of *El Pueblo de Los Angeles* and California was about to be broken when a group of American settlers took over the town of Sonoma on June 14, 1846, and eventually proclaimed California an independent republic. In the square of Sonoma, they raised the symbol of their revolt, the Bear Flag, made from white and red material, with a grizzly bear standing on his hind legs and a star.[228] At dawn, an angry group of Bear Flag supporters arrived at *Comandante* Mariano Vallejo's adobe home on the Sonoma Square. Vallejo, hoping that he could calm the protesters, at first invited them in for breakfast and wine but the Americans were not dissuaded. They arrested him and his brother-in-law, Jacob Leese, along with two others and left to deliver the prisoners to John C. Fremont, an American military officer and well-known explorer[229] who had encouraged the settlers to declare their independence from Mexico.

On the way, the group stopped off at John Reid Wolfskill's *rancho*. John extended his hospitality to the hungry group who devoured the beef jerky that John Reid had drying on a line outside his tule reed house. Once the group was on its way to Fremont's camp, John Reid jumped on his horse, and traveled to Sonoma to join the Bear Flag Revolt.[230] When Fremont later refused to accept Vallejo and the other prisoners, they were taken to Sutter's Fort where they were placed in jail.[231]

On July 7, 1846, Commodore John Drake Sloat, commander of the United States Pacific Squadron, arrived in Monterey harbor.[232] Sloat at first had been cautious about taking over Monterey but in the face of possible military intervention by the British, he demanded the surrender of the *Californios* who did so peacefully. He raised the American flag and issued a proclamation on the plaza in which he promised that the rights of the *Californios* would be protected under the new American laws.[233] However Sloat, 65 years old, ill and ready for retirement, was replaced with Commodore Robert Stockton, a war hawk, who was the opposite of Sloat's more measured approach. As the new head of the United States Pacific Squadron, Stockton had every intention of taking over Alta California through military force.[234]

John C. Fremont joined Commodore Stockton in this aggressive war stance along with his followers, a motley crew of mountain men and impassioned American settlers who supported California's independence from Mexico. Fremont had married Jessie Ann Benton, the daughter of Senator Thomas Hart Benton from Missouri, a Manifest Destiny advocate, who believed that the United States had the right to take over adjoining land as they expanded across the North American continent.

The American takeover snowballed as Commodore Stockton and John C. Fremont became allies. Once Stockton landed in San Pedro,

Governor Pío Pico and General José Antonio Castro, commander of the Mexican forces, tried to negotiate a truce with Stockton who refused and treated them with great contempt, rejecting anything except full surrender. General Castro, furious at Stockton's uncompromising manner sent him a letter stating:

"I will not withhold any sacrifice to oppose your intentions; and if through misfortune, the flag of the United States waves in California, it will not be by my acquiescence nor that of the last of my compatriots."[235]

Faced with Stockton's unyielding stand and fearing an overwhelming American military response, Governor Pico and General Castro decided that a successful fight against the invaders would not be possible. Both men fled Los Angeles for Mexico rather than surrender to the Americans. On August 13, 1846, Stockton and Fremont entered the newly conquered Los Angeles accompanied by a brass band.[236] The residents did not resist but instead eyed the Americans with distrust.

William, who had stayed out of the fight between the *Californios* and the Americans, swore his "faithful allegiance to the United States of America" on September 19, 1846, and promised to serve as a "*regidor* or common Councillor in the *Ciudad de Los Angeles* without fear, favor or affection."[237] Though William was a Mexican citizen, the Americans had taken over the pueblo, and he would abide by their laws.

However, dislike of the American occupation deepened under the strict governance of Archibald H. Gillespie, a marine, who had been appointed military commander of Los Angeles by Stockton. Gillespie antagonized the residents of Los Angeles by threatening unfair punitive action and imposing a restrictive curfew.[238] Outraged by Gillespie's heavy-handed tactics, a group of *Californios* attacked Gillespie's men. *Californio* José María Flores and his soldiers, encouraged by this show of resistance, forced Gillespie to surrender Los Angeles with Flores proclaiming a message of defiance to the pueblo on October 1, 1846:

...We the inhabitants of the department of California, as members of the Great Mexican nation, declare that it is, and has been, our wish to belong to her alone, free and independent...[239]

Gillespie and his men retreated to San Pedro where on October 4, 1846, they sailed for Monterey in Northern California.[240]

For weeks William and Magdalena had told the children that they must stay indoors because of the on-going skirmishes. Magdalena had her hands full with her three youngest children who were all under the age of five. It was especially difficult because her daughter, Madalena, born in May, was only five months old.

"*Niños*, the fighting may be over for a while. Once we know for sure, then you can play outside again. But at the first sound of a gunshot, you must come inside right away and lie down on the floor. Susana and Timoteo, I am counting on you to help your mother in case I am in the fields," said William.

Susana would turn 13 in November and Timoteo was 11.

"Guillermo, is there any word about Pío Pico?" said Magdalena.

"Not much. I've heard he has fled to Mexico but it's only a rumor. He was fair about our land on Putah Creek and he's a good man. Los Angeles will miss him."

William was worried about the lawlessness that was gripping Los Angeles. The Americans under Gillespie had alienated the population, but he wondered how long the *Californios* could withstand the American offensive.

"Mama, I don't like the fighting," said Susana in an unhappy voice. "When will all those soldiers go away?" Magdalena gave her young daughter a hug.

"Hopefully soon," she replied.

Alarmed by the turn of events in the pueblo, Stockton sent Captain William Mervine and over 400 men to San Pedro, near Los Angeles, where he landed on October 8, 1846.[241] José María Flores and his small band of men were ready to make life miserable for the Americans. They had a secret weapon that they hoped would protect the pueblo from the American soldiers. Donated by Doña Clara Cota de Reyes, an elderly *Californio* woman,[242] it was a piece of artillery, a bronze four-pounder swivel gun or *pedrero* that had previously been stationed in front of *La Placita* Church and had fired many salutes during special occasions. When Stockton and Fremont had attacked the pueblo in August, Doña Clara and her daughters hid the gun in a cane patch near their residence on Alameda and First Street, just down the way from William's farm on Alameda and Fourth Street.[243] When the *Californios* needed a miracle to repel the Americans, Doña Clara retrieved the swivel gun and offered it to the *Californio* resistance.

Captain Mervine and his men started their march from San Pedro to Los Angeles under dusty and dry conditions. As they marched for hours towards the pueblo, they were harassed by the *Californios* mounted on horseback who sniped at them and used Doña Clara's swivel gun to target the American soldiers with an occasional large blast. Without a lanyard to fire the swivel gun, the *Californio* gunner had to light the gunpowder with the burning end of his cigarette.[244] Using Doña Clara's swivel gun, the *Californios* were able to push the American soldiers back in what became known as "The Battle of the Old Woman's Gun." If Captain Mervine had only known that the

Californios were bluffing and running out of ammunition, he would have been able to take back Los Angeles. But Lady Luck was on the side of the *Californios* for that moment. Worried that that he could not make progress against the insurgents, Captain Mervine turned back to San Pedro with four dead and ten wounded.[245]

On October 23, 1846, Stockton once again sailed into San Pedro and encountered *Californio* forces who fooled Stockton by making their small army seem like hundreds of soldiers.[246] They brought in a group of wild horses that kicked up so much dust it appeared as if they were a large cavalry unit ready to descend on the Americans. Confronted by what he thought was an overwhelming force, Stockton left for San Diego.[247]

Three days later, Flores, now leader of the resistance, became the Governor of California[248] while Stockton plotted how he could reconquer Los Angeles. The pueblo ground to a halt as the populace had to feed the *Californio* army and everyone waited for the Americans to invade the city again.

In January of 1847, Stockton descended upon the pueblo. By then the residents, especially the foreigners, felt that resistance against the American military was doomed. The *Californios* had their swivel gun from Doña Clara, four pieces of artillery, and a howitzer stolen from the Americans but very poor gunpowder, which most likely contributed to their inability to fight against the American soldiers.[249] The *Californios* were defeated in the final two battles of Southern California. At the Battle of San Gabriel, the *Californios'* artillery proved ineffective which led to their defeat on January 8, 1847. The next day, they lost again at the Battle of La Mesa. Afraid of being captured, Flores left for Mexico but first appointed Andrés Pico as head of the *Californio* forces.[250] Unwilling to deal with Stockton who had treated his men with great contempt, Andrés Pico negotiated their surrender with John C. Fremont on January 13, 1847, and signed the

Treaty of Cahuenga. Fremont was generous in his terms allowing the *Californios* to return home without pledging their allegiance to the United States until a treaty between Mexico and the United States had been worked out. They were to receive the same rights as American citizens and were also allowed to leave the country if they wished. In return, the *Californios* were to stop their resistance and surrender the howitzer and Doña Clara's swivel gun.[251] Even though Fremont did not have the authority to negotiate with Pico, the Americans accepted the peace treaty as a way to end the war in California.

William was inspecting the orchards when Magdalena's excited voice interrupted the stillness.

"Guillermo, quick come here. The news is wonderful. The war is over. We just received word that Andrés Pico and the American, John Fremont, have signed a treaty. *Niños*, we will no longer be hearing gun shots like we've heard over the last few months."

"I want to be a soldier when I'm older," declared Timoteo as he grabbed a stick and started shooting.

"Silly brother, you really don't," laughed Susana who grabbed her brother's stick.

"But I wonder what life will be like under the Americans?" Magdalena's voice became more serious. "What will happen to Andrés Pico and José María Flores and all the others?"

"Magdalena, there will be many changes and some will be difficult. The American laws are different from Mexican laws and it will be hard on many people," said William.

As Susana and Timoteo chased each other, William put his arm around his worried wife.

"Come inside and let's celebrate the end of the war."

They entered the adobe and made their way to the dining room where William kept his finest *aguardiente* in an old wooden brandy chest.

"I've saved this bottle for a special day, *mi amor.* Don't be sad." Magdalena tried to smile but her heart was heavy.

"Here's to the end of the war and to the future of California," toasted William.

～๑

PERSONAL OBSERVATIONS AND RESEARCH

Manifest Destiny was the American policy that supported the right of the United States to expand its territory under a moral imperative to bring its values and culture to adjoining geographic areas. United States President James Polk (1845-1849) was an advocate of Manifest Destiny who believed that the United States had every right to take over the Mexican territory of California.

Alta California was not ready for the American military on-slaught. In 1846, it had a small population of approximately 20,000 to 25,000 people, including *Californios,* Native Americans and some foreigners.[252] It also had a minimal military presence. J.M. Guinn, an American historian who wrote extensively about early California history in the late 1800s and early 1900s, stated the following obser-vation about the American invasion of California:

> The Californians, without provocation on their part and without really knowing the cause why, found their country invaded, their property taken from them and their govern-ment in the hands of an alien race, foreign to them in cus-toms and religion.[253]

Throughout his account of the Mexican-American War in California, Guinn tried to maintain a neutral stance on the events as he re-lated both the American and *Californio* sides of the story. However,

I was struck by his observations, which showed sympathy for the *Californios* as well as underscored the more aggressive behavior of the Americans. Commodore Stockton, for example, came across as a brash officer who regarded the *Californios* with disdain.

As we just saw in the first part of this chapter, John C. Fremont was a supporter of Manifest Destiny. However, when the end of the hostilities occurred in California, Fremont played a very important role in brokering a final agreement that allowed the *Californios* to have dignity in defeat. John C. Fremont and Andrés Pico signed the Treaty of Cahuenga at an adobe farmhouse on January 13, 1847. Unfortunately, the original adobe no longer exists having been demolished in 1900. During a visit to *Campo de Cahuenga*, which is located in Los Angeles near Universal Studios, Rich and I viewed the foundation and tiles of the original adobe farmhouse as well as markers for the rest of the foundation hidden under the sidewalk and street. The adobe foundation was discovered beneath Lankershim Boulevard when the Metro Red Line Subway was built.[254]

I also learned the real story behind the Treaty of Cahuenga's magnanimous terms. Bernarda Ruiz de Rodríguez is the unsung hero of the document. An educated woman from a respected *Californio* family, Bernarda met Fremont in Santa Barbara on December 27, 1846, when Fremont made a stopover en route to Los Angeles. Bernarda asked for and was granted a 10-minute meeting with Fremont where she made an impassioned plea for a just treaty if the Americans won the war in California. Bernarda had four sons fighting on the *Californio* side, and she convinced Fremont that he would have more allies and fewer enemies if he treated the *Californios* with generosity instead of harshness. She encouraged him to free prisoners, give the *Californios* the same rights as American citizens and grant a pardon to Andrés Pico, the head of the *Californio* army.[255] Her 10-minute visit with Fremont extended into a two-hour discussion about the possible terms of a treaty. Bernarda prevailed and was the only woman present when John C. Fremont and Andrés Pico signed the Articles of Capitulation later known as the Treaty of Cahuenga.[256]

After Bernarda's death, Fremont acknowledged her influence, writing in his memoirs in 1887:

> I found that her object was to use her influence to put an end to the war, and to do so upon such just and friendly terms of compromise as would make the peace acceptable and enduring... And she wished me to take into my mind this plan of settlement, to which she would influence her people; meantime, she urged me to hold my hand, so far as possible. Naturally, her character and sound reasoning had its influence with me, and I had no reserves when I assured her I would bear her wishes in mind when the occasion came, and that she might with all confidence speak on this basis with her friends.[257]

Though people may not be aware of her influence, Bernarda Ruiz de Rodríguez played a key role and helped to spare the *Californios* from more humiliating treatment after the war. What makes this story remarkable is that it was unusual for a woman to be able to negotiate with Fremont during that time when women had very little involvement in politics and public life. My research led to an unanticipated bonus when I discovered that I am related to this outspoken and courageous woman. Her mother, María Ygnacia Lugo de Ruiz, was Magdalena Lugo Wolfskill's aunt[258] and therefore she is my great-great-great-aunt (third great-aunt). Finding an ancestor like this is what makes genealogy so rewarding and exciting.

The Mexican-American War in California also had a large impact on William and his family. Before 1846, William had lived a prosperous life as a Mexican citizen and had learned how to navigate the maze of Mexican regulations and politics. He could speak fluently in Spanish and his children were also all bilingual. His wife, Magdalena Lugo Wolfskill, was from one of the prominent *Californio* families of Santa Barbara, and William was a close friend with many of the leading *Californios* in the pueblo. Having grown up in Missouri, William would find himself with an advantage in that he understood American law, which mystified many of his *Californio* friends. Still it must have been hard for William to watch the pueblo struggle under the transition from a Mexican society to an American community with very different values.

---

226 She is called Madalena de los Angeles on her baptismal record and throughout her life was referred to both as Madalena and Magdalena. *The Huntington Library, Early California Population Project Database, 2006,* baptismal record LA 01583.

227 Warner, Hayes, Widney, *An Historical Sketch of Los Angeles County,* 120.

228 Andrew F. Rolle, *California A History,* (New York: Thomas Y Crowell, 1963), 195-196.

229 Robert D.Parmelee, *Pioneer Sonoma,* (Sonoma: The Sonoma Valley Historical Society: 1972), 16.

230 Ned Wolfskill, *A Few of the Things I Remember as Told Me by My Father, the Late J.R. Wolfskill,* 14.

231 Parmelee, *Pioneer Sonoma,* 16.

232 Starr, *California: A History,* 68.

233 Eisenhower, *So Far from God: The U.S. War with Mexico 1846-1848,* (Norman: University of Oklahoma Press: 1989), 215.

234 Ibid., 215.

235 Albert Wilson, *Thompson and West's History of Los Angeles County,* 42.

236 Eisenhower, *So Far from God: The U.S. War with Mexico 1846-1848,* 216.

237 Higbie Wilson, *William Wolfskill: 1798-1866 Frontier Trapper to California Ranchero,* 179.

238 Rolle, *California A History,* (New York: Thomas Y Crowell, 1963), 198-199.

239 Albert Wilson, *Thompson and West's History of Los Angeles County,* 42.

240 Eisenhower, *So Far from God: The U.S. War with Mexico 1846-1848,* 217.

241 Ibid., 218.

242 The word "Doña" was a title placed before the name of a woman in Spanish-speaking Alta California to indicate respect. Guinn calls her Doña Clara Cota de Reyes throughout the account.

243 Guinn, *A History of California and An Extended History of Los Angeles and Environs*, 131. Doña Clara Cota de Reyes is known by different names including Inocencia Reyes and Ignacia Cota De Reyes. http://www.mysanpedro.org/2011/10/ san-pedro-stories-battle-of-old-womans.html

244 Ibid., 132. The battle which took place at the *Rancho Domínguez* is known as "The Battle of the Old Woman's Gun."

245 Eisenhower, *So Far from God: The U.S. War with Mexico 1846-1848*, 218.

246 Guinn, *A History of California and An Extended History of Los Angeles and Environs*, 134-135.

247 Ibid., 134-135.

248 Ibid., 132.

249 Ibid., 140.

250 Eisenhower, *So Far from God: The U.S. War with Mexico 1846-1848*, 228-229.

251 Guinn, *A History of California and An Extended History of Los Angeles and Environs*, 143.

252 John S.D. Eisenhower, *So Far from God: The U.S. War with Mexico 1846-1848*, 200. Eisenhower estimates that California's population was 25,000 people in 1846. Rolle, *California A History*, 186. Rolle estimates that the population of California was 20,000 people in 1845.

253 Guinn, *A History of California and An Extended History of Los Angeles and Environs*, 126.

254 https://www.theclio.com/web/entry?id=16504

255 Cecilia Rasmussen, "Woman Helped bring a Peaceful End to the Mexican-American War," Los Angeles Times, 5 May 2002, http://articles.latimes.com/2002/may/05/local/me-then5, https://www.theclio.com/web/entry?id=16504

256 Rasmussen, "Woman Helped bring a Peaceful End to the Mexican-American War," And https://www.kcet.org/history-society/in-a-state-of-peace-and-tranquility-campo-de-cahuenga-and-the-birth-of-american

257 Ibid.

258 Bernarda's baptismal record shows that her mother was María Ygnacia Lugo de Ruiz, daughter of Francisco Salvador Lugo. María Ygnacia married José Pedro Ruiz. *The Huntington Library, Early California Population Project Database, 2006*, baptismal record BP 00246.

CHAPTER 12

THE GOLDEN LAND

William's Story

As the pueblo adjusted to life after the war, William's wines and brandy or *aguardiente* were garnering a well-deserved reputation for excellence. In early 1847, William received a visit from Lieutenant Edwin Bryant, a member of John C. Fremont's California Battalion.[259] Lt. Bryant had been present when General Andrés Pico and a delegation of *Californios* arrived at Fremont's camp to surrender and sign the Articles of Capitulation on January 13, 1847.[260] William welcomed the opportunity to take the lieutenant on a tour of the Wolfskill vineyard.

"Would you like to taste some of our excellent wines?" William led the officer through his vineyards and orchards towards his adobe house.

"Mr. Wolfskill, I would be most honored. Your reputation has reached our battalion and your fine vineyard is the envy of Los Angeles," answered Lt. Bryant who had heard from many that he should try the Wolfskill brandy.

William opened the heavy door of his adobe and ushered Lt. Bryant inside who found that the rooms were clean and orderly, which one would expect from a man as industrious and careful as William Wolfskill. In the dining room, wooden beams ran the width of the ceiling and a long table with eight chairs stood in the middle of the room, a testimony to William's many children. William then showed Lt Bryant other areas of the adobe and offered him three or four samples of his wine.

"Mr. Wolfskill, your wines could rival the best of the French and Madeira wines."[261]

"Here let me give you some of my favorite peach brandy. Don't mind if I have some myself." William poured two glasses and handed one to the officer.

Bryant savored the brandy and then exclaimed, "May I congratulate you on its excellent flavor."

William poured Lt. Bryant several other samples.

Nothing could please William as much as a compliment to his fine brandy.

"Lt. Bryant, you are welcome to come back any time and have more of this fine *aguardiente*. *Salud* and good luck to you." William and Bryant raised their glasses in a final toast.[262]

Dining Room at the "Old Adobe"
Courtesy of Elena Wolfskill Thornton

In addition to the political changes in the pueblo, the new year of 1847 brought financial problems to William. He wrote on January 22, 1847, to John Reid that times were "unsettled" and that he and his friend, Lemuel Carpenter, had lost over one-third of their crops.[263] He also lamented that he could not send John any more cattle later in the year.

Up to this point, William had helped his brother by sending cattle, seeds, tools and many necessary items for John Reid's new farm, but now with William's crop failure, money and resources were not as abundant.

Mid-year, William received an offer to buy his vineyard and with it the possibility that he could start a whole new life and take his family up to the *rancho* in Northern California. Adventure had filled his youth and perhaps now would be the last opportunity to experience a change. Besides, William and Magdalena really missed John Reid. William wrote:

Dear Brother

...I have a chance to sell the vineyard for $10,000 now. I want your advice which you think would be the best to sell or not. You know if I sell that I have no place to go to except your ranch. If you wish me to not sell please lease out the ranch and cattle and come down here... we have no peaches this year but plenty of pears, grape crops are poor... Doña Rafaela, Madalena and all the children wish to see you...

Your affectionate brother,
William Wolfskill[264]

William did not sell the vineyard or move to Northern California. Instead, he and Magdalena welcomed the birth of their second son, Luis, who was baptized at the Plaza Church on February 10, 1848.[265] Alexander Bell and his wife, María de las Nieves Guirado, once again officiated as *padrinos* or godparents.

In early 1848, William could not foresee that California was about to be swept with gold fever. In January of that year, James Wilson Marshall discovered gold along the American River near present-day Sacramento. Found accidentally as Marshall and his men were building a mill, gold brought thousands of adventurers to California who hoped to find riches and start a new life. San Francisco had only about 800 inhabitants in 1848 but jumped to over 25,000 residents by 1850[266] with most of the new arrivals heading out to the gold fields. Susan Cooper, who later became John Reid Wolfskill's wife, claimed that she had been one of the first to see Marshall's gold when he stopped at her family's house in Benicia in early 1848 and stayed the night en route to San Francisco. She described how they looked "in wonder" as Marshall had taken the gold out of a small rag and declared that he was sure that he had found gold in the riverbed.[267]

William missed his brother and continued to encourage him to leave Northern California and live with them in Los Angeles. But John was very busy up north establishing his own *rancho*. When William heard that John was having trouble walking and riding, he wrote again and begged his brother to get on a ship and come south telling him that "you will find one of the best of receptions from myself and family."[268] Instead, John wrote to his brother of his unhappiness about the *Rancho Río de los Putos* being only in William's name. William responded by writing:

Dear Brother

...Am sorry to hear of your being so unhappy as you appear to be from the stile in which you write me. You appear to be doubtful in respect to a title to your part of the ranch. Now I can settle that as you can have a title to one half of it any time. The reason for my not giving it when up there was becus I did not think there was any person in authority to give it...[269]

The following year on August 27, 1849, William gave John Reid Wolfskill title to half of *Rancho Río de los Putos* in exchange for the sum of $5,000.[270]

That same year William sent his wine up to San Francisco.[271] Fueled by the Gold Rush population explosion in 1848 and 1849, the need for food and other necessities by the gold miners increased dramatically in Northern California. In addition to his wines, Wolfskill also shipped many boxes of grapes via steamer to San Francisco, as did the other grape growers in Los Angeles since fresh fruit was more in demand than wine in Northern California during that time.[272]

William was fortunate to have as a neighbor, Jean Louis Vignes, a Frenchman and wine maker originally from the Bordeaux area in France. He started his winery, *"El Aliso,"* in 1837.[273] Called Don Luis by his *Californio* neighbors, Jean Louis Vignes was known for his fine wines. He was also recognized for planting the first orange grove in Los Angeles with trees from the San Gabriel Mission in 1834. By 1850, much of the orange crop in Los Angeles came from the San Gabriel Mission or from the orchards of Wolfskill or Vignes.[274] Both men were pioneers in the development of the citrus industry, which was still in its infancy. But whereas William sold most of his oranges,

Jean Louis mainly raised his crop for consumption at home or for friends.

In 1851, William visited Jean Louis Vignes, admiring his friend's grape arbor which was about ten feet in width and stretched from the house a quarter of a mile down to the Los Angeles River.[275] Vignes' vineyard and winery, *"El Aliso,"* was named after the towering sycamore tree that provided shade to his wine cellars. This sycamore was over 60 feet tall and spread its branches out almost 200 feet wide. Dating from the days before the arrival of the Spaniards and Mexicans, this imposing tree had been an important meeting place for the Tongva tribe. *El Aliso* is the Spanish word used to designate an Alder tree but in Alta California it was often used in error to refer to Sycamore trees. [276]

A portly man with an amiable face and pork chop sideburns, Jean Louis brought out two glasses and poured his finest red wine for his fellow vintner and friend, placing the glasses on the wrought iron table sitting on the veranda.

"William, I have been saving this bottle for a special occasion. You of all people will appreciate this red since it has been aging in my cellar for several years. *Salud.* To your good health."

As they both raised their glasses in a toast, William was curious about this special occasion.

"I have decided to sell my land." Jean Louis hesitated, took a deep breath and continued.

"I am 71 years old and getting too old to keep working so hard. Here is what I have written up about my property hoping to entice someone to buy it."

Jean Louis took a piece of paper from his pocket, unfolded it and read aloud:

"There are two orange gardens that yield from 5,000 to 6,000 oranges in the season. The vineyard, with 40,000 vines, 32,000 now bearing grapes, will yield 1,000 barrels of wine per annum, the quality of which is well known to be superior."[277] Jean Louis sighed.

"But I am really hoping that my nephews, Pierre and Jean Louis Sainsevain, will buy it from me.[278] They are both hardworking young men who have been very helpful. Ah, my friend, it is hard to think of life without my vineyard but I will always have my wine!"

William was jolted by this announcement. He had always admired Jean Louis' ability to grow about anything on his land from grapes to oranges, to walnuts. He would miss his fellow wine maker and orchardist.

"Your farm is keeping you young. Besides, who can I talk to when I run into problems?" said William.

"You flatter me but your success is growing every day. My wines are wonderful but your *aguardiente* is in a class by itself. Here's to our vineyards, my friend," said Jean Louis.

"To our vineyards but I hope you'll change your mind. You would be sorely missed," said William.

And the two friends and wine makers raised their glasses once again as they toasted the vineyards and their vines laden with grapes.

The year 1851 brought great joy to the Wolfskill family with the birth of Magdalena's last child, María Rafaela, who was baptized in November of 1851 and named after Magdalena's mother, Doña Rafaela Romero de Lugo who lived with the Wolfskill family. Tragically, little María Rafaela died in March of 1855 when she was only 4 years old.[279]

The decade of the 1850s brought William Wolfskill wealth and fame as his vineyard and orchards grew in both size and productivity. He experimented with growing different varieties of fruit, introducing sweet almonds and persimmons to California.[280] His orange groves grew from the initial two acres planted in 1841 to eventually over 70 acres.[281]

Wolfskill Farm Orange Orchard
Rare Books Department Photos Archives
Courtesy of the Huntington Library, San Marino, California

Wolfskill's orchards had many admirers, including Emily Hayes who became a frequent visitor. Judge Benjamin Hayes, Emily's husband, was a lawyer and judge who arrived in California in 1850 from Missouri to establish a new life and law practice in the pueblo.[282] Emily followed him several years later in February 1852 after a journey that took her from St. Louis, Missouri, to Cuba and Panama, where she crossed the Isthmus riding side-saddle on a mule, and continued on to California.[283]

One day in February of 1852, Magdalena told William about Emily's visit to the orchard that morning.[284]

"William, I had a wonderful day today. Emily Hayes came by and we walked through the orchards together. She just arrived from St. Louis and told me about her trip here. Emily particularly liked Havana and its elegant palm trees.[285] She's quite an adventurous person to come all the way from Missouri. She was traveling on boats for 43 days."

"What's Emily like?" asked William. "Two years of separation from the judge must have been difficult for her."

"She's finding the difference from her life in Missouri a bit hard. She still can't get over living in a house made out of mud."[286] Magdalena laughed. "I told her the adobe would become her best friend. The house will stay cool in the summer and warm in the winter. But I don't know if she believed me. Anyhow, the farm has never looked more beautiful than today. The peaches and quince trees were in bloom and the orange trees were full of fruit."[287]

"Did she buy any?" William inquired.

"Yes, she loves oranges. So we picked two dozen and I sold them to her for a dollar.[288] We had a lovely walk but her health is delicate. I hope she's fine. She seems like such a nice person."

"The Judge is a good friend and I hope we'll be close to Emily as well," said William.

In 1854, after a long struggle through the courts, William Wolfskill received an order from the United States Land Commission on November 7 that *Rancho Río de los Putos* in Northern California finally belonged to him. William thought back on the time nine years earlier when Governor Pico had settled his land dispute with

Juan Manuel Vaca and Juan Felipe Peña. William had waited nine long years and now the land grant had finally been confirmed by the courts.[289]

In 1854, William rescued the newly established public school on Spring Street that had shut down due to a shortage of money. Supportive of education, William paid the bills for about six months until the city treasury could come up with the money to fund it.[290]

In 1855, William bought out a nursery of orange and lemon trees owned by Dr. Halsey for $4,000. In 1857, he added several thousand orange trees establishing the largest citrus orchard not only in Los Angeles but in the United States.[291]

July of 1856 brought more changes to *Rancho Río de los Putos*. William decided that he no longer would maintain a part in the Northern California property that he co-owned with his brother, John Reid, and sold his half interest to his brother, Mathus Wolfskill, Edward McGary, Andrew Stevenson, and G.B. Stevenson for the price of $71,000. Several years later, the land was sold back to John Reid Wolfskill with Mathus Wolfskill keeping 870 acres.[292]

Starting with her first visit to William's farm in 1852, Emily Hayes returned often to buy fruit from the Wolfskills over the next five years. In September of 1857, William walked through the vine-yards and thought back on Emily's visit of just two days earlier. He had given her some peaches and a bottle of grape juice, which she always loved and when she came back the next day, he gave her more peaches. Judge Hayes had remarked how improved Emily seemed after her long walks out to the Wolfskill place.[293] Happy with wandering through the orchards, she was one of the nicest visitors to the farm. But William was concerned about her health.

"Magdalena, I have some very sad news." He put his arm around his wife. "Emily Hayes died last night."[294]

Magdalena looked at her husband in total disbelief. "Why she was just here two days ago! How can she be dead?"

"They haven't said what she died from.[295] How sad for her young son to lose his mother," said William.

"She never seemed happy here. Also she didn't want her husband to run for Judge and hated it when he campaigned. But I still can't believe she's gone. How terrible." replied Magdalena, shaken by the news.

"I was always worried about her. She seemed so delicate," said William.

Magdalena made the sign of the cross and prayed for the young woman who so loved to visit their orchards.

By 1858, William had about 30 orange trees that were older and filled with fruit as well as 2,050 orange trees that were not bearing yet and 1,000 orange trees in his nursery. He was also growing citron, lemon and lime trees, pears, walnuts, apricots, apples, olives, figs, and peaches.[296] That year, the Wolfskill farm was visited by a committee from the California State Agricultural Society which reported that in addition to his vineyards and citrus orchards, William was growing a variety of other fruit trees such as peach, pear, plum and cherry trees. The report complimented him:

"Perhaps no man in the fruit business of this state has realized a more complete and satisfactory success than the proprietor of this place."[297] However, starting in 1857, William had to battle an invasion of bugs, "a species of Aphis" that affected the citrus trees and caused a drop in his crop.[298]

Famous for his orchards, William also delighted in his very successful vineyards. Throughout the years, he added more vines until he had over 55,000 vines in 1858.[299] The year 1859 brought further success as William was awarded "$30.00 for the best vineyard at the State Fair... $25.00 for the best three-dozen oranges, and $35.00 for the best orange and walnut groves..."[300] Not only did he win prizes for his vineyards and orchards, William had a banner year selling 449,000 pounds of grapes for $337,000.[301]

The production of wine and fine brandy or *aguardiente* was at the top of William's priorities for his vineyard. H.D. Barrows, employed by William as a teacher for his children, sailed to New York on the steamship *California* in September, 1857 with gifts for President Buchanan and took along a "barrel of fine old California port, made by Mr. Wolfskill from his own vineyard."[302] For a man who had arrived penniless in the pueblo in 1831, it showed how far William had traveled to be able to send his port wine to the President of the United States.

~◦

PERSONAL OBSERVATIONS AND RESEARCH

Los Angeles is currently a thriving metropolis with millions of residents, so it is hard for us to imagine that the pueblo was a small, agricultural town of around 2,200 inhabitants in 1836.[303] Even when it became an incorporated city in 1850 under the Americans, Los Angeles was still a rural town with few amenities. J.M. Guinn, a local historian, described Los Angeles in the following manner:

> There was not a sidewalk nor graded street within its bounds; not a street lamp nor a water pipe—not a school house nor a post office; not a printing press nor a newspaper. It owned no municipal buildings—not even a jail. It had a church and a graveyard, neither of which belonged to the city; and yet these were the only public improvements (if a graveyard can be called a public improvement) that seventy years of *ayuntamiento* rule had produced.[304]

H.D. Barrows wrote in his *Reminiscences of Los Angeles in the Fifties and Early Sixties:*

> We had no railroads in those days, nor telegraphs, prior to 1860; steamers arrived twice a month at our only port, San Pedro, bringing us mails and news from the outside world to partially relieve our isolation.[305]

After the Mexican-American war was over in California in 1847, *El Pueblo de Los Angeles* transitioned from being under Mexican rule to living under American laws. In his article "The Passing of the Old Pueblo," J.M. Guinn wrote in 1901 that:

> The process of Americanizing the people was no easy un- dertaking...The native population neither understood the language nor the customs of their new rulers, and the new- comers among the Americans had very little toleration for the slow-going Mexican ways and methods they found pre- vailing in the city."[306]

Spanish remained the dominant language of Los Angeles for many years. The *Muy Illustre Ayuntamiento* or Very Illustrious City Council that had disbursed justice under Mexican rule was replaced in 1850 with the Los Angeles Common Council. Yet, the laws of the city council continued to be published in both English and Spanish until the mid- 1870s because so many of the city's inhabitants spoke only Spanish.[307]

William Wolfskill and his family were bilingual and prospered under the Mexican as well as the American regimes since William was familiar with both sets of laws. Others were not so lucky and many prominent *Californio* families eventually lost their land and their wealth under the American takeover.

William was a businessman and multiplied his earnings as a farmer by loaning money out. His ledgers from the 1840s and 1850s are still in the Wolfskill family's possession and read like the who's who of *El Pueblo de Los Angeles*. Names like Manuel Requena, Governor Pío Pico, Jean Louis Vignes and Abel Stearns show that the top citizens came to William to borrow money. One of the most illustrious borrowers was Miguel de Pedrorena from San Diego County who borrowed money in 1843. Born in Burgos, Spain, in January of 1808,[308] Miguel was one of eight Hispanic signers of the California Constitution in 1849. Miguel was also considered one of the founders of the City of San Diego. Highly educated and entrepreneurial, he died suddenly on March 31, 1850[309] where upon his estate borrowed money from William to cover Miguel's funeral expenses.[310] He was land rich and cash poor as many found themselves after the Mexican-American War. Miguel de Pedrorena is my great-great-grandfather. Elena de Pedrorena, his daughter, married Joseph Wolfskill, William's son, in 1869, uniting the Wolfskill and de Pedrorena families.

Miguel de Pedrorena
Courtesy of Elena Wolfskill Thornton

During this time, William's letters to his brother, John Reid Wolfskill, continue to help us understand how the brothers worked together to build their *Rancho Río de los Putos*. One particular letter written on August 10, 1847 surprised me when I read that William considered selling his land in Southern California and moving to their Northern California ranch. William was struggling with his business, but his decision to stay in Los Angeles led to his great success later on. Though I do not have the letter with John Reid's response, I can imagine that John wanted to maintain his independence from his older brother and did not want William and his family to relocate to Northern California. John Reid was diligently working to build his own legacy.

John Reid's success in establishing *Rancho Río de los Putos* encouraged several Wolfskill brothers to come out West. Milton Wolfskill, the youngest sibling, lived in Missouri until 1848 when he joined a caravan of prospectors and made the long journey to California in hopes of finding gold.[311] Mathus Wolfskill and his family traveled from Missouri to California in an ox-drawn wagon arriving in 1850 while Sarchel Wolfskill followed in 1852 with his family after crossing the Isthmus of Panama.[312] All three brothers settled in or near Winters in Northern California upon their arrival.

---

259 Edwin Bryant, *What I Saw in California* (1848, Reprint, Minneapolis, Ross and Haines, Inc., 1967), 412. This scene is based on an eyewitness account by Edwin Bryant in *What I Saw in California* where he gave details about his visit to the Wolfskill farm.
260 Ibid., 392.
261 Ibid., 412.
262 Ibid.
263 Letter to John Reid Wolfskill from William Wolfskill, January 22, 1847, The Huntington Library, San Marino, California, The Wolfskill Collection.
264 Letter to John Reid Wolfskill from William Wolfskill, August 10, 1847, The Huntington Library, San Marino, California, The Wolfskill Collection.

265 *The Huntington Library, Early California Population Project Database, 2006*, baptismal record LA 01810. Luis was also called Lewis when he was older. I have chosen to call him Luis throughout the book since that is the name that a number of his descendants call him.

266 Rolle, *California: A History*, 211.

267 "The Foremothers Tell of Olden Times," The Chronicle, San Francisco, September 9, 1900. http://www.sfmuseum.org/hist5/foremoms.html Susan Cooper Wolfskill's letter is after the letter by Mrs. F.A. Van Winkle. Accessed 12-28-15.

268 Letter from William Wolfskill to John Reid Wolfskill, June 5, 1848, The Huntington Library, San Marino, California, The Wolfskill Collection.

269 Letter from William Wolfskill to John Reid Wolfskill October 3, 1848, The Huntington Library, San Marino, California, The Wolfskill Collection.

270 *Rancho Río de los Putos* Title document recorded in Vol. A, page 369 Records of Benicia, California, August 28, 1849, The Huntington Library, San Marino, California, The Wolfskill Collection.

271 Albert Wilson, *Thompson and West's History of Los Angeles County*, 65.

272 Ruth Teiser and Catherine Harroun, *Winemaking in California* (New York: McGraw-Hill Book Company, 1983), 21.

273 https://www.kcet.org/shows/lost-la/el-aliso-ancient-sycamore-was-silent-witness-to-four-centuries-of-la-history

274 Colonel J.J. Warner, Judge Benjamin Hayes, Dr. J.P. Widney, *An Historical Sketch of Los Angeles County*, 112.

275 Newmark, *Sixty Years in Southern California: 1853-1913*, 197.

276 https://www.kcet.org/shows/lost-la/el-aliso-ancient-sycamore-was-silent-witness-to-four-centuries-of-la-history

277 Albert Wilson, *Thompson and West's History of Los Angeles County*, 35.

278 Jean Louis and Pierre Sainsevain eventually became very famous wine producers.

279 *The Huntington Library, Early California Population Project Database, 2006*, baptismal record LA 00530 and death record LA 00201.

280 Colonel J.J. Warner, Judge Benjamin Hayes, Dr. J.P. Widney, *An Historical Sketch of Los Angeles County*, 76-77.

281 Higbie Wilson, *William Wolfskill: 1798-1866 Frontier Trapper to California Ranchero*, 149-150.

282 Newmark, *Sixty Years in Southern California: 1853-1913*, 46.

283 Benjamin Hayes, *Pioneer Notes* (Los Angeles: Published by Marjorie Tisdale Wolcott 1929), 85-87.

284 Ibid., 87. This scene is based on information in Emily Hayes' journal and her letters to her sister.

285 Ibid., 85.

286 Ibid., 88.

287 Ibid., 87.

288 Ibid., 87.

289 Ogden Hoffman, Reports of Land Cases Determined in the United States District Court (San Francisco: Numa Hubert, Publisher, 1862) 32.

290 Willis Blenkinsop, "A Better Country in Which to Settle: A Biographical Sketch of William Wolfskill," in *The Westerners Brand Book 16*, ed. Raymund F. Wood, (Glendale: The Westerners, 1982), 52.

291 Newmark, *Sixty Years in Southern California: 1853-1913*, 211-212.

292 Higbie Wilson, *William Wolfskill: 1798-1866 Frontier Trapper to California Ranchero*, 141.

293 Hayes, *Pioneer Notes*, 166.

294 Ibid., 166-167. Emily Hayes died in the evening of September 12, 1857. This scene with William and Magdalena is based on Judge Hayes' observations.

295 There is no mention of the cause of Mrs. Hayes death in "Pioneer Notes: From the Diaries of Judge Benjamin Hayes."

296 H.D. Barrows, "Wolfskill's Vineyard and Orchard at Los Angeles: The Story of a California Pioneer," *San Francisco Daily Evening Bulletin, December 17, 1858.*

297 Higbie Wilson, *William Wolfskill: 1798-1866 Frontier Trapper to California Ranchero*, 159. "Report of the Visiting Committee" Transactions of the California State Agricultural Society for 1858 (Sacramento, 1859), 239.

298 John S. Hittell, *The Resources of California*, Third Edition, (San Francisco: A. Roman and Company, 1867), 193.

299 Barrows, "Wolfskill's Vineyard and Orchard at Los Angeles: The Story of a California Pioneer."

300 Higbie Wilson, *William Wolfskill: 1798-1866 Frontier Trapper to California Ranchero*, 175. Los Angeles Star November 1, 1859.

301 Ibid.

302 Albert Wilson, *Thompson and West's History of Los Angeles County*, 65.

303 Los Angeles City Archives, Register of the City of Los Angeles and Its Jurisdiction Year 1836, 532. Men: 603, Women: 421, Children: 651, *Indios:*(Indians) 553.

304 J.M. Guinn, "The Passing of the Old Pueblo," *Historical Society of Southern California*, (Read December 1901): 113-120.

305 H.D. Barrows, "Reminiscences of Los Angeles in the Fifties and Early Sixties," *Historical Society of Southern California*, (1893): 55-62.

306 Guinn, "The Passing of the Old Pueblo," 116.

307 Ibid., 120.

308 Matthew Hovius, *The Ancestry of Miguel de Pedrorena*, (2007) a genealogy study in Spain commissioned by Conchita Thornton Marusich. According to the records of the Parish church of San Roman in Burgos, Spain, Baptisms, Book 1775-1831, Miguel de Pedrorena was baptized in Burgos, Spain on January 6, 1808.

309 San Diego Mission, Burials III. Father Holbein officiated at the funeral on April 1, 1850.

310 William Wolfskill, *Ledger of Accounts 1840-1850*, Wolfskill Family, 125, 184, 185.

311 Higbie Wilson, *William Wolfskill: 1798-1866 Frontier Trapper to California Ranchero*, 140.

312 "Winters Express" Reprint from the *1975 Centennial Edition of the Winters Express.*

CHAPTER 13

WILLIAM WOLFSKILL'S SUCCESS GROWS

William's Story

In the mid-1850s, Los Angeles continued to feel like a Mexican town even though it was part of the United States. To its north, stood the majestic San Gabriel Mountains while to its south rolled an endless basin. Bright red-tiled rooftops sat like crowns on the earth-colored adobe buildings constructed with mud and straw. Gardens were filled with roses, oleanders and crepe myrtle. An agricultural town, the pueblo distributed water from the Los Angeles River through the *Zanja Madre* or Mother Ditch to a series of smaller ditches or *zanjas* carrying water to the gardens, orchards and vineyards that filled the land. The plaza, a large open space, was the center of the town. On one side was the Catholic Church, Our Lady of the Angels, or, *Nuestra Senora de los Angeles*, the biggest and most prominent building in the area.[313] It stood like a guard over the families who had built their adobe homes around the plaza when Los Angeles was under Mexican rule.

Living on the outskirts of the pueblo, William was busy on his 100-acre farm making wine, cultivating award-winning orange orchards and raising his large family. A supporter of education, he started a school in his adobe in order to home school his own children as well as children of his family, friends and neighbors. During one of his trips to Northern California in 1854 to see his brother,

John Reid, William met a young teacher, Henry Dwight Barrows, known as H.D. Barrows, and convinced him to come south and teach at the Wolfskill school. After accepting the job, H.D. traveled with William from San Francisco on the steamer *Goliah*. They arrived in San Pedro on December 12, 1854, and finished the journey to Los Angeles on a stagecoach.[314]

Though William had received little formal education, he was a lover of books and felt very fortunate to have such a fine tutor working in his home. The Wolfskill children had studied with other teachers, but H.D. Barrows was the most outstanding of them all—smart, well-educated and a fine musician. William's children ranged in age from Timoteo, a teenager, to his six-year-old son, Luis.

Wanting to share his school with others, William invited his brother Mathus' son, John Wolfskill, from Suisun in Northern California to live at his adobe in Los Angeles. He also extended the invitation to several of his friends including John Rowland's two sons as well as Lemuel Carpenter's children, María Refugio and her brother Francisco.[315] In 1856, J.E. Pleasants, also known as Ed, was invited to come from Northern California to live with the Wolfskills. Ed's family members were neighbors of John Reid Wolfskill and had met William during his visits to his *Rancho Río de los Putos*. Since there were no schools close to their home, young 17-year-old, Ed, seized the opportunity to come south and live with the Wolfskill family.[316]

The classes were held in English and Spanish, with an emphasis on reading the classics and surveying for the older boys. A gifted musician, Barrows taught his students the piano and flute as well as other instruments.

During the summer of 1856, Barrows took Timoteo Wolfskill and Ed Pleasants to spend a week in early July at the old San Fernando Mission that had been turned into General Andrés Pico's summer home. The San Fernando Mission had survived many changes. It had been under the Franciscan order since its establishment in 1797 but the mission's religious affiliation ended when it was secularized in 1834. The secularization of all the Alta California missions had officially started in 1833 under orders from the Mexican government who wished to end the religious affiliation of the missions and redistribute the land from the missions to the Indians and to newly arrived Mexican settlers.[317] Later on, Governor Pío Pico leased the mission to his brother, General Andrés Pico,[318] who used it as a summerhouse.

Barrows and his students arrived at the San Fernando Mission on July 2, 1856.[319] Surrounded by distant mountains on all sides, the mission was located on a barren, almost desert-like plain. The tops of tall elegant palm trees towered above the outside walls that surrounded the mission buildings. Inside the travelers found an abundant garden of orange, lemon and olive trees made possible by irrigation. The adobe buildings, which were constructed in a rectangle around the garden patio, included the church, a long colonnade with numerous workshops and the monastery or *convento* where the friars or padres lived. H.D. Barrows, Timoteo and Ed slept in the guest rooms of the monastery and were greeted every morning by the "cheerful" songs of wild birds.[320]

The favorite activity of the young students was riding with the cowboys or *vaqueros* while they looked after large herds of cattle grazing out on the range. One of their most vivid experiences happened early one morning during the cattle drive back to the mission before sunrise. Ed described the moment as pure poetry:

> The rugged peaks of the Sierra Tujunga slowly emerged from the shadow of the night, tinted rose and purple; and as the stars faded from sight, a bank of cloud behind them turned to rose, then to gold, and the whole plain and the mission buildings just coming into view, were flooded with a transparent golden light.[321]

The rodeo on July 4th turned out to be another highlight for both boys. Hesitant at first and unsure if they were skilled enough to be part of the festivities, Timoteo and Ed rode on the "gentle saddle horses" and soon were helping the cowboys put on the rodeo.[322]

Andrés Pico was famous for his hospitality and excellent cuisine. The dinners were all five- and six-course meals featuring *Californio* and Spanish food served on bone china plates by waiters. A trio of musicians playing harp, guitar and violin in the background further enhanced the dining experience. Young Ed Pleasants particularly enjoyed their renditions of "dreamy Spanish airs" which were most welcome after a long day of cattle herding and riding on spirited horses.[323] When their visit at the San Fernando Mission was over, H.D. Barrows and his two students headed back to the "Old Adobe" filled with many wonderful memories of their stay with General Andrés Pico.

Sadness came to the Wolfskill school in 1859 when Lemuel Carpenter, María Refugio's father, encountered financial difficulties. Lemuel was born in Kentucky and came over the Old Spanish Trail after William's expedition. He married María Domínguez who was related to Magdalena Lugo Wolfskill and eventually bought the approximately 21,000-acre *Rancho Santa Gertrudes* from his wife's aunt. Lemuel worked hard building up a soap factory and the *rancho* but he also loved horseracing and the good life. In order to pay for his high life style, Lemuel had borrowed $5,000 in 1852 from John Downey, who would later become the Governor of California, and James McFarland, his business partner. With interest at 2% per month compounded monthly, the loan ballooned out of control until Lemuel owed $104,000 by 1859. Deeply in debt to his creditors, he was forced to sell his beloved *Rancho Santa Gertrudes* to pay off his loan. Lemuel couldn't take the pressure anymore and finally shot himself in the head on November 5, 1859, just days before the sale.[324] His creditor, John Downey, picked up *Rancho Santa Gertrudes* at the sheriff's sale when it went up for auction to pay off the loan.

Devastated by the loss of her father, María Refugio stayed at the "Old Adobe" that Christmas as her classmates tried to help her through her sadness. On January 3, 1860, María wrote in her diary:

The day was very clear but towards the evening the clouds began to gather. Last night I saw my father in my dream.[325]

The next day the Wolfskill children attempted to raise María Refugio's spirits. Juana played the piano and later both Luis and Joseph dressed up as girls[326] to make María laugh which helped to distract her. But by the following evening on January 5, María was again sad and homesick.[327] She could not believe that her father was gone and that she would never see him again.

The year 1860 brought more changes to the "Old Adobe." Cupid worked his magic and delivered great happiness to the family. Juana Wolfskill, now 19 years old, fell in love with her teacher, H.D. Barrows, a 35-year-old bachelor, who won Juana's heart and hand in marriage. They were married on November 14, 1860.[328] They started their married life with adventure as they took the Butterfield Stagecoach from Los Angeles, California, on December 17, 1860, to St. Louis, Missouri. Covering about 2,391 miles and traveling day and night for more than 18 days,[329] Juana and H.D. Barrows were confined with seven other passengers in a lightweight coach, which accentuated every bump in the road. Warned by the Butterfield Stage Company that people traveled at their own risk, every passenger carried some type of firearm or knife to be used in case of attack. The beauty of the landscape and the excitement of traveling compensated for the strenuous conditions of the trip. Barrows announced at the end of the journey: •

To many people, doubtless, who think more of their ease than they do of robust physical health, a stage ride of a thousand or two thousand miles, may seem a very formidable undertaking. But for those who had a liking for adventure, and a desire to see something of the world, a long ride of two or three weeks, practically in the open air, not in hot, stuffy cars, possesses a wonderful charm, especially in remembrance...[330]

In 1860 while looking for a large area to graze cattle, William bought the *Rancho Lomas de Santiago* encompassing approximately 47,200 acres or eleven leagues from Don Teodosio Yorba and Doña Inocencia Reyes de Yorba for the amount of $7,000.[331] Don Teodosio, an old friend of William's, was known for his hospitality and generosity but was in bad health and ready to sell his ranch. A Mexican land grant, *Rancho Lomas de Santiago* was granted in 1846 to Teodosio Yorba by Governor Pío Pico with the following boundaries: the mountains on the east, *Rancho Aliso* on the south, the Santa Ana River on the north and *Rancho San Joaquin* to the west.[332]

The next year in 1861, William sent Ed Pleasants, 22 years old, down to *Rancho Lomas de Santiago* to be in charge of his cattle operations. Young and enthusiastic, Ed loved the wide-open spaces and spent most of his time keeping a watchful eye on Wolfskill's cattle and horses, since there were no fences to keep the animals from wandering.[333]

William's workmen were in the middle of building a house on *Rancho Lomas de Santiago* near present-day Irvine Park, when two men from the Yorba family arrived on horseback. They informed William's carpenters that they were mistakenly building on the Yorba's other property, *Rancho Santiago de Santa Ana* which they owned with their cousins, the Peraltas. Not to be deterred, William immediately approached some of the Yorba and Peralta family members and bought shares of *Rancho Santiago de Santa Ana* allowing William to graze his cattle on an even larger area.[334]

The next several years were difficult on a personal level for the Wolfskills. María Susana, William's first-born child with Luz Valencia, died in 1861 at the age of 28.[335] During that same year, Magdalena, William's wife, became sick and soon had trouble taking care of herself.[336] In early 1862, Juana wrote to her brother, Timoteo, in Mazatlán, Mexico, that Magdalena's health had deteriorated and that she had been sick for two months with cramps.[337]

Magdalena continued to experience increasing pain.

"*Mi amor*, how do you feel today?" said William, concerned that his wife was not getting better.

"Guillermo, I want to be here with you and the family. But the doctors can do nothing for me," said Magdalena as she closed her eyes. William could see the nagging pain reflected in her face. He knew that she was worried about the family and how they would cope if she died. It was hard for him to see her suffering so much.

"Guillermo, you are as strong as an ox. I know you'll be fine and will take good care of the family when I am no longer on this earth."

For a brief moment, her eyes were shining bright with love and respect for her husband. And when the pain returned, she turned away so that he would not see her agony.

"Magdalena, you must fight this illness. I need you." William pleaded with her but knew in his heart that she did not have the will to continue.

On July 5, 1862, the family was summoned to the "Old Adobe" because Magdalena had taken a turn for the worse. William and Doña Rafaela, Magdalena's mother, were there at her bedside when all the children arrived to be with their mother. María Refugio Carpenter had been out dancing all night when Joseph Wolfskill found her and brought her home to be with Magdalena and the family.[338] As the day wore on, the pain became more acute and the doctors could do nothing for her. William watched the love of his life starting to slip away. Finally just after midnight on July 6, surrounded by her family, Magdalena passed away. Calm at the end, she was prepared for death. William and Magdalena's mother, Doña Rafaela, were both overcome by emotion and became sick[339]while the rest of the family stayed at her bedside and held a "watch" with the body all night.[340]A "likeness" or death mask was taken of Magdalena's face.[341]

The news of Magdalena's death spread throughout the pueblo. On Monday, July 7, the funeral procession started from the "Old Adobe" around 9 o'clock in the morning. The men were on horseback and the women walked in a procession as they accompanied Magdalena's body to the church on the plaza where a mass was said in her memory.[342] At her funeral, Reverend B. Raho read from St Paul's first epistle to the Thessalonians Chapter 4, verses 13-17 talking about how those who have died "will have a part in the Second Coming." Poor William was lost without his sweet, supportive wife who had been by his side since 1841. Only 58 years old at her death, Magdalena was described in her obituary as having the virtues of "a lost mother, a beloved wife and estimable friend."[343] The procession proceeded to the Catholic graveyard on the hill where Magdalena was buried. When they returned to the adobe, William and the family experienced a great "heaviness" and felt that all the rooms had a "vacant" look.[344]

Only 10 days after her mother's death, Juana gave birth to a baby girl on July 16, 1862.[345] Little Alice Wolfskill Barrows brought much joy to the Wolfskill home and helped to ease some of the pain from Magdalena's death. But within two to three weeks, Juana developed a nagging cough. Only 22 years old, she became weak and did not improve which prompted H.D. Barrows to write Timoteo in August that he was "anxious" about Juana's cough.[346] The doctors were unable to help her, and William was in despair at the thought of losing his young daughter. The months dragged on with her cough becoming worse. Overtaken by her illness, Juana passed away in H.D. Barrows' arms on January 31, 1863.[347] Her funeral was held in the plaza church where she had been baptized and where her mother only six months earlier had been laid to rest.

A survivor in the face of adversity, William continued to care for his remaining family members who ranged in age from Luis, the youngest who was 15, to Timoteo, the eldest, who was now 28 years old and living in Mexico. Considered part of the family, H.D. Barrows remained close to the Wolfskills.

~~

PERSONAL OBSERVATIONS AND RESEARCH

One of the joys of researching William Wolfskill has been finding newspaper stories, letters and diaries from the 19th century, which have given me a better sense of William and his family. H.D. Barrows wrote a number of newspaper articles and short accounts about William that are tantalizing bits and pieces that leave us wanting more information. Barrows' articles on other historical figures, including John Reid Wolfskill and Juan José Warner, offer important information about these early California pioneers. He also authored numerous reminiscences about the early days of *El Pueblo de Los Angeles* which give us insight into the city's transition from its Native American and Mexican roots to its Americanization. In addition to his essays, Barrows wrote many letters to Timoteo Wolfskill in Mazatlán, Mexico, which give us details about William, Magdalena and Timoteo's siblings.

H.D. Barrows
Courtesy of Joan Hedding

J.E. Pleasants, a prolific writer, left us a treasure-trove of letters and articles about his time with the Wolfskill family. His numerous manuscripts and photos are among the Pleasants Family Papers, which now reside in the Special Collections and Archives at the UC Irvine Libraries with some of the material being available online in a digital format.[348] The Pleasants Family Papers have been a valuable resource during my research on the Wolfskills. I refer to J.E. Pleasants as Ed in my book since that is the name that his family and friends called him.

J.E. or Ed Pleasants
Courtesy of UC Irvine Libraries, Special Collections
and Archives, Pleasants Family Papers

The diaries and letters of María Refugio Carpenter, who married Ed Pleasants, are also archived in the Pleasants Family Papers at UC Irvine. Young María Refugio wrote a series of diaries from 1860 until 1865 that give us an insight into her life as well as her interaction with the Wolfskill family during that time.[349] For example, I learned information about the last days and death of Magdalena Lugo Wolfskill in María Refugio's diary entries that I had not read anywhere else, underscoring the importance of reading old letters and journals as we search for clues to our ancestors' past. Frances Meadows, wife of well-known Orange County historian, Don Meadows, transcribed María's diaries that were written in pencil in small and often difficult-to-read script. Frances also wrote footnotes to the sparsely written diary entries that provided important background on the people and events mentioned in Maria Refugio's journals. The facts that I learned from María's 1862 diary and Frances Meadows' footnotes enabled me to write the detailed account of Magdalena's last days and death described earlier in this chapter.

María Refugio Carpenter
Courtesy of UC Irvine Libraries, Special Collections
and Archives, Pleasants Family Papers

In addition to reading old newspapers, diaries and letters, I have also found references to William Wolfskill in books and novels. Imagine my surprise upon reading Louis L'Amour's *The Lonesome Gods* when William Wolfskill's name popped up in the conversation of one of the main characters of this book. L'Amour, a popular Western writer, uses William Wolfskill as a symbol throughout this book to represent the "forward thinking men" of Los Angeles. For example, Miss Nesselrode, the heroine of the story, encourages the young orphan she is caring for to make something of his life by following the example of certain community leaders like William Wolfskill.[350] In another chapter, L'Amour has the well-known mountain man, Peg-Leg Smith, stating that Wolfskill's orchards and vineyards will make him a rich man.[351] Louis L'Amour caught the essence of William Wolfskill, a visionary who built his success on hard work.

313   J.E. Pleasants, "Los Angeles in 1856" *Touring Topics* (January, 1930): 36.

314   Barrows, "Los Angeles Fifty Years Ago" *Historical Society of Southern California* (1905): 203.

315   Higbie Wilson, *William Wolfskill: 1798-1866 Frontier Trapper to California Ranchero*, 190.

316   William McPherson, "Joseph Edward Pleasants," manuscript, Pleasants Family Papers. Special Collections and Archives, The UC Irvine Libraries, Irvine, California.

317   Starr, *California: A History*, 47-48.

318   California's Missions, ed. Ralph B. Wright (Los Angeles: California Mission Trails Assn., LTD, 1950), 78.

319   J.E. Pleasants, "A Fourth of July at San Fernando Mission in 1856" from a handwritten manuscript pages 1-13, Pleasants Family Papers. Special Collections and Archives, The UC Irvine Libraries, Irvine, California, 2.

320   Ibid., 6.

321   Ibid., 10.

322   Ibid., 2.

323   Ibid., 7,8.

324   Frances Meadows, *The Diaries of Mary Refugio Carpenter of Los Nietos: 1860-1865*, from a manuscript in the Don Meadows Papers in Special Collections and Archives, UC Irvine Libraries, Irvine, California, 4.

325   María Refugio Carpenter's diary 1860, January 3, 1860, Pleasants Family Papers. Special Collections and Archives, The UC Irvine Libraries, Irvine, California.

326 Ibid., January 4 1860.

327 Ibid., January 5, 1860.

328 Newmark, *Sixty Years in Southern California: 1853-1913*, 142.

329 H.D. Barrows "A Two Thousand Mile Stage Ride," *Historical Society of Southern California, Los Angeles (1896)*: 40.

330 Ibid., 44.

331 Robert Glass Cleland, *The Irvine Ranch of Orange County* (San Marino, California: The Huntington Library, 1952), 52-53. Terry E. Stephenson, *Shadows of Old Saddleback: Tales of the Santa Ana Mountains*, 44-45.

332 Cleland, *The Irvine Ranch of Orange County*, 52-53. Originally a Mexican land grant, *Rancho Lomas de Santiago* was granted in 1846 to Teodosio Yorba by Governor Pío Pico who gave him four leagues or approximately 17,700 acres. However, the boundaries listed in Governor Pío Pico's land grant actually entitled the Yorbas to 11 leagues or approximately 47,200 acres, which is the acreage that William purchased from Yorba. By the time the land grant was patented in 1868 and confirmed by the U. S. Land Commission, the land was calculated at 11 leagues instead of the original four leagues.

333 McPherson, "J.E. Pleasants Biography," 6-7.

334 Stephenson, *Shadows of Old Saddleback: Tales of the Santa Ana Mountains*, 44-45.

335 Newmark, *Sixty Years in Southern California: 1853-1913*, 171.

336 Letter from H.D. Barrows to Timoteo Wolfskill, August 26, 1862, Amy Wolfskill Smith Collection.

337 Letter from Juana Wolfskill Barrows to Timoteo Wolfskill, February 27, 1862, Amy Wolfskill Smith Collection.

338 María Refugio's 1862 diary Saturday, July 5, 1862, Pleasants Family Papers.

339 Ibid., Sunday, July 6.

340 Footnote 25 in a manuscript by Frances Meadows for María Refugio Carpenter's 1862 diary. "Watching," sometimes called "waking" is a custom of sitting with the body of the deceased until burial.

341 Refugio's 1862 Diary, Sunday, July 6, 1862

342 Footnote 26 in a manuscript by Frances Meadows for María Refugio Carpenter's 1862 diary.

343 Obituary, Los Angeles, July 10, 1862. I found Magdalena's obituary in Elena de Pedrorena's (my great-grandmother) mass missal.

344 Refugio's 1862 Diary, Monday, July 7, 1862.

345 Letter from H.D. Barrows to Timoteo Wolfskill, August 26, 1862, Amy Wolfskill Smith Collection.

346 Ibid.

347 Higbie Wilson, *William Wolfskill: 1798-1866 Frontier Trapper to California Ranchero*, 196. H.D. Barrows, "Diary," January 31, 1863.

348 Guide to the Pleasants Family Papers, Online Archives of California http://www.oac.cdlib.org/findaid/ark:/13030/tf967nb619/ Accessed on12-28-15.

349 Ibid.

350 Louis L'Amour, *The Lonesome Gods* (Toronto, New York, London, Sydney: Bantam Books, 1983), 164.

351 Ibid., 48-49.

LETTERS TO TIMOTEO

Wolfskill Family Story

William Wolfskill's Children
Left to Right: Unknown Woman,
José, Magdalena, Francisca and Luis
Courtesy of Michele Stephenson

Sometime between 1859 and 1861, Timoteo Wolfskill, William's eldest son, moved to Mazatlán, Mexico, far away from his family in the pueblo. His departure from Los Angeles caused William, Timoteo's siblings and H.D. Barrows to write him numerous letters inquiring about his life in Mexico as well as imploring him to come home.

Through these letters, his brothers and sisters kept Timoteo informed of the important events in the Wolfskill family as well as in the pueblo.

Timoteo Wolfskill
Courtesy of Amy Wolfskill Smith

William sent a letter on May 13, 1861, addressed to Timothy Wolfskill Esq. in Mazatlán, Mexico, in which he was critical towards Timoteo who had asked him for money. He seemed worried that Timoteo was going to spend his money foolishly on some type of risky business venture or speculation.

Timoteo my dear boy

…In answer to your request for money I think from what Mr. Yorba tells me you are much more flush than I am at present as he tells me you have 3000 or 4000 thousand dollars on hand. And I say even if you have not so much I know you have plenty for all your necessities or present purposes excepting your wish to go into some speculation which you know I do not approve of…

Yours affectionately Wm Wolfskill[352]

Several letters to Timoteo were about Magdalena's and Juana's health problems as we saw in the last chapter. H.D. Barrows gave an update to Timoteo on August 26, 1862, informing him that:

…Doña Magdalena has died. She departed this life about midnight of 5th and 6th July after a long and painful illness about a year of which she was unable to help herself…Her death was a great affliction to the family especially to your father and Doña Rafaela although it was expected.

Barrows also let Timoteo know that Juana had given birth to their daughter, Alice Wolfskill Barrows. He described Juana's health after the birth with concern, writing:

Juana gave birth to a daughter on the 16 of July—10 days after her mother's [Magdalena's] death. She got along very well for 2 or 3 weeks but since, she has had a cough and has been quite weak... I feel anxious about her cough...

Barrows finished the letter by saying:

Write often and come home as soon as you can. ...I hope you won't go and get married down in Mazatlán.

Truly Your Friend
Henry D. Barrows[353]

Juana Wolfskill Barrows
Courtesy of Joan Hedding

The letters to Timoteo are filled with the affection and respect that his brothers and sisters felt towards Timoteo and are very heartwarming. Throughout 1863, they begged him to return to Los Angeles. On August 1, Barrows wrote:

> We were all glad to hear from you again the other day to hear that you thought some day of coming home...[354]

On August 7, Timoteo's brother and my great-grandfather, Joseph, mentioned in his letter how much William and the family enjoyed hearing from Timoteo. He closed the letter saying:

> I heard you was about to get married. If so, I hope you have picked out a good and loving wife. I hope you will come home soon...
>
> I remain yours truly,
> Joseph Wm Wolfskill[355]

José or Joseph Wolfskill
Courtesy of Elena Wolfskill Thornton

January 29, 1863, brought a letter in Spanish to Timoteo from Manuela Furman living in San Francisco who addressed him as

"Mi querido hermano" which means in English "My dear brother."[356]
I believe that Manuela Furman is the married name of Manuela
Valencia, daughter of Luz Valencia, William's common-law wife.
Manuela was listed as part of the Wolfskill household in the 1836
City of Los Angeles Register.[357] This was quite a revelation since
Manuela Valencia Furman is never mentioned in any history books
about the Wolfskill family. What happened to Manuela and why did
she disappear? I believe that Luz Valencia took Manuela with her
when she left William Wolfskill in 1836 and probably when she accompanied Francisco Araujo to Mexico in 1837.

There is a very curious letter dated August 3, 1863, from San
Francisco, supposedly written by Joseph Wolfskill to Timoteo asking him to send money to Manuela. It is written in very bad English
with multiple misspellings and does not sound like Joseph's other
letters which reflect a high knowledge of English:

> Manuela sends to you horse(her) best respects. All hear(her)
> children is well ...she needs money and I haven't got it and of
> cose(course) she most (must) call on you for thar(there) is no
> budayelse (nobody else)...
>
> I cannot rought (write) to you any more.
> Joseph Wolfskill[358]

We do not know who wrote this letter or why it is attributed to
Joseph. Perhaps it was written by Manuela or someone close to her
since it is an urgent appeal for money for Manuela.

H.D. Barrows sent a letter to Timoteo on March 30, 1864:

> You wrote some time ago about paying over some of your
> money here to Manuela, your sister, but I did not know

anything about where she could be found and so could not do anything as I did not know who to inquire about her... Write often.

Truly your friend
H.D. Barrows[359]

This letter from H.D. Barrows shows that Manuela did not seem to have contact with the Wolfskill family except with Timoteo since Barrows was very close to the whole family and would have known Manuela or at least have had information on how to locate her. It is the last time we hear about Manuela until almost a decade later.

In 1864, there are several letters to Timoteo from his brother, Luis, who was frustrated by his father's reluctance to pay for him to go to school. In January, Luis wrote to Timoteo complaining:

My father won't send me to a school where I can learn any [thing]. I have asked him several times but he says that he can't afford to send me and I think there is a pretty good show for me to grow up an ignoramus... When do you think of coming home again? We would like to see you very much....[360]

Then in June, Luis again complained that his father had considered sending him to school but changed his mind.

Luis or Lewis Wolfskill
Courtesy of Joan Hedding

Francisca Wolfskill, William's oldest surviving daughter, shared good news with Timoteo on January 11, 1865:

Luis went to San Francisco before New Year; he is going to school. I hope he will get on well with his studies. He wanted to learn so much. I wish I had an opportunity of going to school or at least of learning music really well but there is no hope. There are a good many things that we have to give up in this life but I think I could be perfectly happy if I was a good musician. I do love music...

...Do write to me soon - all about yourself and sweet heart. Tell me what she is like. And now Brother goodbye and God bless you.

From your sister
Francisca[361]

Francisca Wolfskill
Courtesy of Michele Stephenson

This letter is significant for a number of reasons. We learn that Luis finally is allowed to go to school. We also get a glimpse into Francisca Wolfskill's dreams that she too would like to attend school and study music. It is interesting that William fostered a love of learning among his children through home schooling but seemed reticent about letting them go on to regular educational institutions. Women in the 1860s were especially limited in pursuing higher education since they were regarded as wives and mothers and therefore not needing too much education.

In 1865, Luis sent several letters letting Timoteo know how he was doing in school. In March, he wrote:

> I tell you I worked hard to get off to school. I had been trying for 3-4 years but thank God I am now in school and I will do my best.

He ended the letter asking, "How are you doing in mining. I hope you will do well."[362]

By October, Luis reported that he had moved schools and was now studying in Oakland, which wasn't as "noisy" as San Francisco.

On April 25, 1867, Victor Furman who appears to be related to Manuela wrote to Timoteo asking for information on Mexico:

> My Dear and Honored Uncle,
>
> I inform you of my poor health. I think of going to Mexico... My father left here two years ago for New York and we have not heard of him since. The family is all well. Dear Uncle, I wish you would inform me of that country. I would like to

spend two or three years down there. Please excuse my writing for this is the first letter I have undertaking.

Yours Nephew
Victor Furman[363]

In a letter written on January 9, 1868, Joseph, turned down Timoteo's appeal for financial help after William's death in 1866:

…You say you wish I should help you in your affairs. I am sorry to tell you that at present it is impossible for me to help you. My means are not very great, besides I have to help my brother Luis as it was a request my father asked of me before he died and therefore I have to do so with Luis. As regards to the rest of the family, Frances is in school in San José, Luis is living on a ranch name is *Santa Anita*. Madalena is living close to town with her husband and she has two children, a boy and a girl. I am living on part of home place which was given to me. The other part to Frances…You must not think hard of me because I cannot help you. I have the family to look after besides myself…

I remain your affectionate brother,
J.W. Wolfskill[364]

The last letter in this series to Timoteo came on January 5, 1873, from his sister, Manuela Furman. The letter was written for Manuela in English by William Furman, whose identity remains unclear:

Dear Brother

I am very glad to hear that you are married and got a wife in all manners as you desired. I am very thankful for the money that you sent me as it came just in an hour of need as I was then over heels in debt...Please give my best respects to your wife and you and [have] her send your photographs and the names of the children and their photographs...Wishing you a "Happy New Year" I close

Your Affectionate Sister
Manuela[365]

Manuela's letter provides us small clues into Timoteo's world. This is the first time that we learn that Timoteo was married, had children and was still living in Mexico. The fact that he sent Manuela money in her time of great financial need speaks to Timoteo's character, sense of generosity and loyalty to family. Unfortunately Manuela's letter gives us little information about her life and she remains the mystery Wolfskill half-sister.

Manuela's letter written in 1873 wraps up the Letters to Timoteo during the 1860s and 1870s that provide so many valuable details about the Wolfskill family.

~~

PERSONAL OBSERVATIONS AND RESEARCH

In this chapter, we learned more about the Wolfskill family through letters that family members and friends wrote to Timoteo. Whereas the rest of the book focuses primarily on William's and Magdalena's story, this chapter introduces us to William's grown children who share their hopes, disappointments and successes in addition to shedding more light on William and Magdalena through their letters. The only voice missing from these letters is Timoteo's since unfortunately, I have never found any of his letters.

I am a descendant of Joseph or José Wolfskill who was William's second oldest son. I was born in California but raised in New York as well as New Jersey and I remember hearing a lot about our Wolfskill family. When I moved to Los Angeles after college, I finally met Joseph Wolfskill's descendants who live mostly in Southern California. It wasn't until I moved to Napa in Northern California that I met the descendants of William's other children and was very fortunate to meet my cousins who are descendants of Luis Wolfskill, William's youngest son. Avid genealogists, my cousins opened their hearts to me and passed on many of their wonderful family recollections. Among the treasures that they shared was a copy of the letters written to Timoteo Wolfskill by his siblings, father and H.D. Barrows. These letters were preserved by Amy Wolfskill Smith and loaned to me by her daughter, Marguerite Oates.

Timoteo, William's eldest son, appeared to be William's most independent and adventurous child. Whereas the other Wolfskill siblings settled in Los Angeles, Timoteo went to Mazatlán, Mexico, to find his future and fortune. Timoteo seemed to be more of a risk taker and had been interested in mining before he moved to Mazatlán. Ed Pleasants, described a trip where he and Timoteo went prospecting for gold on the Gila and Colorado rivers in 1859. Ed wrote:

Tim and I were boys just out of school and ready for adventure. We were well equipped with a good camp outfit, consisting of a light lumber wagon, four good mules, mining tools, provisions for the trip and grain for the team.[366]

After five months, Ed Pleasants and Timoteo each ended up with a $500 profit in gold for their work. Then Timoteo left for Mexico. Some of the Wolfskills wonder if Timoteo ever encountered his mother, Luz Valencia, who left for Mazatlán in 1837 with her husband, Francisco Araujo, William and Luz's silversmith neighbor. I wonder what happened to the descendants of Manuela and José de la Cruz Araujo who could have been William's son.

To help the readers keep track of William's children, I have made the following chart that outlines William's children with Luz Valencia, his common-law wife, Luz Valencia's children where the father is unknown and William's children with Magdalena Lugo:

VALENCIA AND WOLFSKILL CHILDREN

William Wolfskill

Common-Law Marriage:

1. **Luz Valencia**

Children:

1. **María Susana Valencia Wolfskill**: christened 18 November 1833 in Los Angeles, California
2. **Timoteo Valencia Wolfskill**: christened 30 January 1835 in Los Angeles, California

Children (father unknown)

1. **Manuela Valencia**: christened 2 January 1829 in Los Angeles, California

2. **Petra Valencia**: christened 6 July 1832 in San Gabriel, California
3. **José de la Cruz Valencia**: christened 3 June 1836 in Los Angeles, California

Marriage

1. **Magdalena Lugo:** 12 January 1841 in Santa Barbara, California

Children:

1. **Juana or Juanita Josefa Wolfskill**: christened 23 November 1841 in Los Angeles, California
2. **María Francisca Wolfskill**: christened 13 June 1843 in Los Angeles, California
3. **José or Joseph Wolfskill**: christened 15 September 1844 in Los Angeles, California
4. **Madalena de los Angeles or Magdalena Wolfskill**: christened 13 May 1846 in Los Angeles, California
5. **Luis or Lewis Wolfskill**: christened 10 February 1848 in Los Angeles, California
6. **María Rafaela Wolfskill**: christened November 1851 in Los Angeles, California

As for Timoteo, many in the Wolfskill family would like to know what happened to him after he moved to Mexico. I have not found any documentation that Timoteo returned to the pueblo. It must have been hard for Timoteo to learn after William's death that his father had divided up his extensive estate and given all of his children and grandchildren property but left nothing to him. William had always appeared to be a fair person so it was sad and surprising that William excluded his oldest son. Perhaps he was hurt that Timoteo stayed in Mazatlán instead of returning to the pueblo.

Over the past several years, Pamela Storm, whose children are descendants of Timoteo, has unearthed important information. Her findings about various members of the Wolfskill family and Timoteo's descendants can be seen online in the Wolfskill Family Scrapbook.[367] According to Pamela, the original letters to Timoteo from his family and H.D. Barrows were eventually passed down to Richard Henry Wolfskill who received them from his father, Marcos Wolfskill, Timoteo's grandson. We know that Timoteo married Melchora Lizarraga in Mexico and moved to Copala, Mexico, near Mazatlán where his first son, Guillermo, was born. Copala is a charming old silver mining town. I discovered through some documents in Spanish on the Internet that in 1888, Timoteo was involved in the San José mine in Copala[368] and that by the early 20th century, the family owned over 22 mines in Concordia, Mexico[369].

In 2016, I made contact through social media with one of Timoteo's descendants in Mazatlán, Mexico, who gave me some information on Timoteo's son, Guillermo. I had made several inquiries on social media to different Wolfskills in Mexico, but it took a year before someone responded to me. When I finally received a response, I was excited to discover a link to the Mexican Wolfskills. The Internet and social media websites are all great tools in any search for family descendants, but it can take time to find your clues from reliable sources. In genealogy research, it is important to never become discouraged and to keep persevering until you find your answer. My hunt for information about Timoteo and his descendants will be ongoing as I continue my research.

---

352   Letter from William Wolfskill, Los Angeles, May 13, 1861.

353   Letter from H.D. Barrows, Los Angeles, August 26, 1862.
354   Letter from H.D. Barrows, Los Angeles, August 1, 1863.
355   Letter from Joseph Wolfskill, Los Angeles, August 7, 1863.
356   Letter from Manuela Furman, San Francisco, January 29, 1863.
357   Los Angeles City Archives, *1836 City of Los Angeles Register*, 465 and 466.
358   Letter signed Joseph Wolfskill, San Francisco, August 3, 1863 but perhaps is from Manuela Furman.
359   Letter from H.D. Barrows Los Angeles, March 30, 1864.
360   Letter from Luis Wolfskill, Los Angeles, January 23, 1864.
361   Letter from Francisca Wolfskill, Los Angeles, January 11, 1865.
362   Letter from Luis Wolfskill, San Francisco, March 19, 1865.
363   Letter from Victor Furman, San Francisco, April 25, 1867.
364   Letter from Joseph Wolfskill, Los Angeles, January 9, 1868.
365   Letter from Manuela Furman, San Francisco, January 5, 1873.
366   J.E. Pleasants, "A Mining Trip to Colorado in 1859," Pleasants Family Papers. Unpublished Manuscript, MS-R044. Special Collections and Archives, The UC Irvine Libraries, Irvine, California, 1.
367   http://pamelastorm.com/wlf_a.htm
368   *Inventario del Archivo Municipal de Concordia, Sinaloa*, 2009, 26. http://www.adabi.org.mx/content/descargas/inventarios/220_concordia_sin.pdf
369   *Crecimiento y Crisis de la Minería en Sinaloa 1907-1950*, Universidad Autónoma de Sinaloa, 24. http://historia.uasnet.mx/maestria/archivos/tesis/15/tesis%20francisco%20osuna.pdf

CHAPTER 15

THE CALIFORNIA DROUGHT

William's Story

California was unprepared for what turned into one of the worst droughts in the state's history starting in 1863. Joseph Wolfskill wrote to Timoteo on August 7, 1863:

> This has been a very bad year for stock...The stock is commencing to die off. God knows how many will die if the worst time has not come yet...[370]

In the summer of 1863 while visiting his mining interests in Ivanpah in the East Mojave Desert, William noticed grassy areas that ran 20 to 30 miles long and one-half to a mile wide along the Mojave River bottom area.[371] When the rains still did not come at the end of 1863 and his cattle were in danger of starving to death from lack of food, William decided to send young Ed Pleasants down to the Mojave with about 2,000 head of cattle and 300 horses. He also asked his friends, William Workman and John Rowland, who owned *Rancho La Puente* if they wanted to join his expedition and transfer their 3,000 head of cattle and several hundred horses to the Mojave. Billy Rowland, a former student at the Wolfskill school, was sent to help Ed and six cowboys accomplish the move. Transporting a large herd of over 5,000 cattle was difficult so they took 500 head of cattle at a time.[372]

They started the transfer in January of 1864 and traveled only about 15 miles per day since the cattle were thin from lack of food and grazing was poor along the route. Ed Pleasants reported that one of the toughest parts of their journey occurred when they crossed the Cajon Pass and became engulfed in a sleet storm. It was so cold that icicles hung from the horses' bridle bits. The two young men and the cowboys kept pushing their herd through the sleet, as they made their way over the rocky, desolate Cajon Pass. Finally during their descent, the sleet lessened and the wind lost some of its sting. They eventually reached the river where their animals were able to find some decent grazing land.[373] Ed and his group continued along the Mojave River and set up camp down river from present-day Victorville and about 25 miles from Camp Cady,[374] a government post built in the early 1860s on the Mojave River to protect the US mail and government troops.[375]

On January 23, 1864, Luis Wolfskill wrote to Timoteo:

There has been no rain here for two years and there hasn't been any grass either. The stock is dying off very fast. Don Abel has lost 5,000 or 6,000 of cattle by starvation.[376]

Don Abel Stearns was one of the most prosperous men in the pueblo, but he suffered the loss of 30,000 head of cattle during the drought.[377] By mid-March of 1864, Ed Pleasants and Billy Rowland had transferred approximately 5,000 head of cattle and hundreds of horses.[378]

Six months later, Luis again reported to Timoteo about the drought:

Ed has moved the stock from the ranch to the mohave river because there is no grass and I think he will move them further on where there is more grass. A great deal of stock died this year by starvation. We didn't lose much.[379]

Ed Pleasants and Billy Rowland stayed in the Mojave Desert for more than a year as the drought continued to decimate hundreds of thousands of cattle throughout the state of California. Even though the rains began in the fall of 1864, Ed and Billy stayed in the desert and waited to bring their herds back to Los Angeles until April of 1865. Because of the difficult nature of the cattle drives between Los Angeles and the Mojave Desert, William Wolfskill lost about 25% of his cattle. But he counted himself lucky because most other ranchers who did not move their cattle out of Los Angeles lost 75% percent of their herds.[380]

After the drought, the ranching landscape of Southern California was vastly different. The ranchers had to borrow heavily against their ranches to pay bills causing many owners to go bankrupt since their cattle had died and their source of income dried up. By April of 1864, 50,000 cattle were sold at the Santa Barbara Auction for only about $.37 per head which was an enormous drop from 1862 when cattle were selling for $8-$12 per head.[381] Before the drought, the cattle industry had been the foundation of the economy but by 1865, agriculture had replaced it, or as Ed Pleasants wrote, Southern California became "a land of orchards instead of a vast stock range."[382]

Wolfskill's friend, Ignacio del Valle, was a victim of the devastation in cattle prices. Ignacio, who had served as mayor or *alcalde* of Los Angeles for a short time, was part owner of the *Rancho San Francisco* located in present-day Newhall, California. He planted the first large orange orchards in Ventura County on his *rancho* from tree seedlings from William's farm in the pueblo. Unfortunately, Ignacio's stepmother, Jacoba Felix de Salazar, owned another part of the *rancho* and with cattle prices plummeting had buried herself in debt. She borrowed against the land, owing $8,500 to William Wolfskill and almost $8,000 to other creditors. Afraid that he would lose his part in the *rancho* due to Jacoba's loans, Ignacio made an appeal to William Wolfskill to save him by taking over the other mortgage debt that his stepmother had incurred. To help Ignacio out, in 1864 William filed for foreclosure on the *Rancho San Francisco* and bought the property for $16,350 at the sheriff's sale for the sum of the debt. He then deeded five-elevenths of the *rancho* to Ignacio del Valle who was freed from his stepmother's financial problems.[383] In 1865, William and Ignacio decided to sell the land to Thomas Bard for $53,320 with $21,307 going to Wolfskill. The rest went to Ignacio and his brother, José, who also owned an interest. Convinced that there was a large deposit of oil under *Rancho San Francisco*, Thomas Bard transferred the land to the Philadelphia and California Petroleum Company. Bard also sold 1,300 acres back to Ignacio del Valle for $500 so that he could continue to live on his ranch.[384]

Joseph Wolfskill wrote to Timoteo on March 16, 1865:

The great cry is oil now. Everybody is looking for pitch springs. The *Rancho of San Francisquito*[385] has a great deal of pitch on it. Father had a mortgage on it. The ranch came into his hands, had 5 leagues in it. He sold it to these oil men for $21,000.00. I hope that those oil companies may succeed for it will be of great benefit to Los Angeles County.[386]

The drought brought another property to William Wolfskill. *Rancho Azusa*, a 6,500 acre property, belonged to Andrés Duarte, a former Mexican military officer who had received his land grant in 1841.[387] When Duarte could not make his mortgage payments, William foreclosed on the ranch and bought it at the sheriff's sale for $4,000 in December of 1863.[388] Luis Wolfskill inherited the land after William's death.

William Wolfskill's final acquisition was his purchase of the beautiful *Rancho Santa Anita* in 1865, another victim of the drought. William paid $20,000 for 11,319 acres to Dibblee, Corbitt, and Barker who had purchased the land to graze their cattle.[389] Devastated by several years of drought that decimated their herds, the three co-owners were ready to sell. Once William owned *Rancho Santa Anita*, he planted the first eucalyptus trees in California from seeds brought over from Australia.[390] When William died in 1866, his son, Luis, inherited the *rancho*, which he later sold to Harris Newmark, a successful Los Angeles merchant, in 1872 for $85,000.[391] What seemed at first a disastrous decision for Newmark who suffered some business setbacks that year, the purchase of the *Rancho Santa Anita* proved fortuitous. Lucky Baldwin bought the *rancho* only three years later in 1875 for the unheard of price of $200,000, paying his first payment of $12,500 in cash from a tin box filled with several million dollars.[392]

In 1866, William Wolfskill sold his *Rancho Lomas de Santiago* in Orange County for $7,000, the same amount he had paid Don Teodosio Yorba for the property in 1860.[393] William sold the land to Flint, Bixby & Company, a group of successful sheep ranchers from Monterey County. Their partner, James Irvine, was part of the purchasing group. The hilly and rocky terrain of *Rancho Lomas de Santiago* was well suited for sheep ranching, and gave accessibility to the Santa Ana River on its northern boundary, thereby providing valuable water rights for the ranchers. Once the Irvine, Flint & Bixby group added the *Lomas de Santiago* acres to their other properties, their land stretched from the ocean to the Santa Ana River and included over 110,000 acres[394] which one day would become the Irvine Ranch.

Personal Observations and Research

California's economy in 1862 was largely based on ranching with cattle selling as high as $8-$12 per head.[395] It had been a banner year for rain, which meant lots of grass for the herds, but starting in 1863, the rain stopped coming. By April of 1864, the price of cattle had plummeted to less than a dollar per animal.[396] Ed Pleasants estimated that not more than 4 inches of rain fell from October 1863 to June 1864. In addition, he wrote that the winds aggravated the situation.

> The southeast wind would start with every favorable indication for rain. It would cloud up and all the rancheros would begin to rejoice in the prospect, when the desert, or so called 'Santa Ana' wind would set in and scatter every cloud on the horizon. This wind would blow for days, parching the already dry ground and shattering the hopes of the stockmen.[397]

The drought permeated the Wolfskill family's life. As we saw in their letters to Timoteo, his siblings wrote to him about the serious lack of rain and its effect on the land. As the drought persisted, William began searching for places where he could graze his cattle including the East Mojave Desert in California. The lifeline of the desert is the Mojave River that has its beginning in the San Bernardino Mountains where it gets its water from the snow pack.[398] It is primarily an underground river though it flows above ground in certain areas such as Victorville, Barstow and Afton Canyon on its way towards the East Mojave Desert and eventually disappears into the sands of Soda Lake near Baker, California. William had traveled through the area back in 1831 on the last part of his journey to San Gabriel, California, and had followed the Mojave Indian trails[399] used for centuries as a trade route.

Rich and I have visited this part of the desert many times. Today, one can drive on the Mojave Road that follows the Old Mojave Indian trails and parts of the Old Spanish Trail. We have taken our SUV along these sections of compacted sand and dirt. Often the road signs are occasional landmarks like deserted fences or collection of stones piled on top of each other called cairns that guide travelers through the lonely desert. Since there are few signs along the Mojave Road, for safety reasons, people who want to follow it for a day or two should take along a book such as *Mojave Road Guide* by Dennis Casebier or *The Old Spanish Trail: Across the Mojave Desert* by Harold Austin Steiner that give very detailed directions and maps.

Mojave Road
Photo by Conchita Thornton Marusich

During the time that I was writing this book, California experienced a terrible drought that went on for several years. Every drop, every weather forecast that predicted rain became cause for celebration, so I viscerally felt what William Wolfskill and his fellow Californians must have experienced when the precious liquid stopped coming.

370   Letter from Joseph Wm Wolfskill to Timoteo, Los Angeles, August 7, 1863.

371   Pleasants, "Tiding Over a Dry Year on the Mojave in 1864," handwritten manuscript, Pleasants Family Papers, Special Collections and Archives, The UC Irvine Libraries, Irvine, California, 4-5.

372   Ibid., 3, 6, 7.

373   Ibid., 7-8.

374   Ibid., 8,12.

375   Casebier, *Mojave Road Guide: An Adventure Through Time*, 22.

376   Letter from Luis Wolfskill to Timoteo, Los Angeles, January 23, 1864.

377   Rolle, *California: A History*, 344.

378   Pleasants, 3, 6. William Wolfskill had 2,000 cattle and Rowland/Workman had 3,000 cattle.

379   Letter from Luis Wolfskill to Timoteo, Los Angeles, June 12, 1864.

380   Pleasants, "Tiding Over a Dry Year on the Mojave in 1864," 19.

381   Albert Wilson, History of Los Angeles County, 57.

382   Pleasants, "Tiding Over a Dry Year on the Mojave in 1864," 21.

383   Ruth Waldo Newhall, *A California Legend: The Newhall Land and Farming Company* (Valencia, California: The Newhall Land and Farming Company, 1992), 58.

384   Ibid., 59.

385   Even though Joseph Wolfskill wrote *Rancho San Francisquito*, he obviously was referring to *Rancho San Francisco* since the amount William sold it for matches with the sale to Thomas Bard.

386   Joseph Wolfskill to Timoteo, Los Angeles, March 16, 1865.

387   Cowan, *Ranchos of California: A List of Spanish Concessions 1775-1822 and Mexican Grants 1822-1846*, 17-18.

388   Blenkinsop, "A Better Country in Which to Settle: A Biographical Sketch of William Wolfskill," 54.

389   http://www.arboretum.org/explore/our-history/ website which explores the history of the Los Angeles County Arboretum & Botanic Garden.

390   Newmark, *Sixty Years in Southern California:1853- 1913*, 439. These original Eucalyptus trees can still be seen at the lagoon at the Los Angeles County Arboretum in Arcadia, California.

391   Ibid., 439.

392 Ibid., 474.
393 Cleland, *The Irvine Ranch of Orange County*, 53.
394 Ibid.
395 Albert Wilson, *Thompson and West's History of Los Angeles County*, 57.
396 Ibid.
397 J.E. Pleasants, "Tiding Over a Dry Year on the Mojave in 1864", 3.
398 Ibid., 5.
399 Steiner, *The Old Spanish Trail Across the Mojave Desert*, 46.

CHAPTER 16

WILLIAM WOLFSKILL'S LEGACY

William's Story

The decade of the 1860s had brought William Wolfskill to the pinnacle of his accomplishments. His vineyards and orchards were famous and profitable while his real estate ventures had increased his land holdings by thousands of acres. In addition, William was the Public Administrator for Los Angeles for the year 1866-67. On a personal note, his children were doing well. In 1865, his daughter, Magdalena, married Frank Sabichi,[400] a prominent attorney in Los Angeles who received his education in Europe. William's sons, Joseph and Luis, were involved with the running of the farm while Francisca was a devoted daughter and lived at the "Old Adobe." H.D. Barrows continued to be close to the Wolfskill family.

But William was slowing down. Several members of the family noted these changes in their letters to Timoteo.

Barrows wrote him on July 13, 1864, that:

Your father grows old -- can't endure as much as formerly -- still he knocks about and goes to town daily.[401]

On October 19, 1865, Luis reported to Timoteo:

Father's health has not been very good for the last year or two.[402]

In early June of 1866, William was not feeling well and started to worry about what would happen if he died without a will. Life on the farm was always busy and there were a million things that took him away from making decisions about how he would want his property distributed. But as each day brought more pain to his body, he realized that his moment of truth had arrived.

William asked that his good friend, H.D. Barrows, stop by so that he could discuss several pressing items with him.

"Henry, I am not strong now and my body is getting weaker every day. I want to make sure that my family is taken care of. So I have decided to have my will drawn up. I'd like you, my son, Joseph, and my brother, Mathus, to oversee the will. I know that you'll all work well together."

"Of course, William. I would be happy to do anything that you ask. You'll get strong again but it's always good to have everything clearly spelled out as to your wishes," responded Barrows alarmed that William might not survive this illness.

"Thanks for being such a good friend to me and to my family. You loved my daughter and faced the sorrow of losing her at such a young age, but I'm glad you still feel part of our family. A good friend is not easy to find."

William was exhausted. As he thought about how to take care of his family, his mind kept sorting through all of his property until he came up with a plan.

He decided to split his main farm, the jewel of his land holdings, between his son, Joseph, and his daughter, Francisca. Joseph had been his right-hand man on the farm and William had the greatest confidence that the farm operations would continue to be successful under his son's guidance. He left Joseph the large Wolfskill Adobe home including "the casks, vats, ...ploughs and farming utensils and stills and the gentle horses and animals used to cultivate said place, together with the orchards, trees..."[403]

Francisca received the remainder of the farm including a number of vineyards and orchards including the Casildo Aguilar Vineyard, the Bernacio Sotelo Vineyard, the Brundige Vineyard, the Ramon Valenzuela Vineyard and the "lands formerly belonging to Louis Lamereaux." William decided to leave his musically inclined daughter the piano from the "Old Adobe," which should make her happy.[404] He smiled as he thought how much Francisca loved music.

Reflecting on his daughter Magdalena, William thought she would do well with several vineyards including a vineyard on the east side of the Los Angeles River that formerly belonged to Vignes and the Mullally Vineyard. He gave her the store called "Apothecaries Hall" as well as a house and lot "just above and to the rear of the Catholic Church." Also musical, Magdalena would receive the mandolin from the adobe as well as his other piano that was being kept at the home of his friend and business associate, Solomon Lazard.[405] He was happy that he could give each daughter a piano. He recalled with fondness how he had brought a piano from New York around the Horn so that his family could enjoy music.[406]

To his youngest son, Luis, William left *Rancho Santa Anita* that he had purchased from Dibblee, Corbitt and Barker. He remembered planting five blue gum or eucalyptus trees from seeds that came from Australia near the old house and hoped that they would tower over the *rancho*.[407] William decided that Luis would do well with *Rancho Azusa* in addition to *Rancho Santa Anita*. Since they were located next to each other, he gave Luis the "gentle stock and farming materials" belonging to both ranches. Finally, he left Luis the eight-day clock from the "Old Adobe."[408]

William then thought of his grandchildren, Willie and Leonora Cardwell, children of his daughter Susana and her husband H.C. Cardwell who had both passed away. William gave Willie and

Leonora a house and lands in San Bernardino called the "Tucker Place" and a store on Main Street known as "Buffum's Drinking Saloon."[409]

He thought about his other granddaughter, Alice Barrows, daughter of Juana Wolfskill Barrows, deceased, and H.D. Barrows. William decided that Alice should get the Scott Vineyard and "five thousand dollars in gold coin."[410] Her father, H.D. Barrows, would hold this property in trust for her.

After much deliberation, William had his will drawn up on June 6, 1866, and distributed his many properties among his children and grandchildren.[411] Solomon Lazard and A.B. Chapman served as witnesses. Being a careful and organized person, William felt better now that his wishes were written down and would be followed after his death.

On September 16, 1866, William suffered a mild heart attack, which caused him to stay in bed for several days.[412] His body was tired and he could hardly walk. Distressed at seeing their father ill, various members of the family stayed by his side at all times and monitored his deteriorating condition.

H.D. Barrows came by to visit William with an important purpose in mind.

"William, we would like to take your picture as soon as possible," said Barrows, in hopes that William would be interested.

"You want my old grizzly face in a picture?" said William. "Let me think about it."

"You've said that before but there is no better time than now," insisted Barrows. "Everyone in the family wants one. And think what joy it will bring to your grandchildren. I'm going to talk to Henri Penelon right now and see when he can bring his camera here. I promise you that it will not take too long."

He waited to see if William would agree. William could be stubborn but Barrows worried that this might be the last opportunity to capture William's picture since he seemed to be getting weaker every day.

"I'll think about it. Maybe I'll do it," answered William.

On September 27, William agreed to have his picture taken by Henri Penelon, a local photographer and artist who had captured images of many of the leading families of Los Angeles in both photographs and oil paintings. It was a warm day, hotter than normal but pleasant.[413] H.D. Barrows and a friend carried William to the north corridor of the adobe where Penelon took the only photograph ever recorded of William Wolfskill.[414]

Only Photo Ever Taken of William
Wolfskill, September 27, 1866
Courtesy of Joan Hedding

175

William was exhausted but thankful that Mr. Penelon had been able to come to the adobe. His children had been asking him for some time to sit for a portrait but life was always just too busy. Now, he had satisfied their requests.

Over the next few days, the pain in his chest became more intense. He could no longer sleep at night, his energy was ebbing away, and he had lost his appetite. Even his favorite drink, *aguardiente,* or brandy no longer appealed to him. It was the deep, incessant pain that dominated his every waking moment.[415]

William finally fell asleep and dreamed of setting out as a young man on a brisk autumn day from Abiquiu, New Mexico, going northward towards the deep canyons of the Colorado River, crossing the snowy mountains of Utah, and traveling westward...

William Wolfskill died on October 3, 1866. H.D. Barrows wrote in his diary:

> Mr. W. died at 8:30 A.M. after a long and useful life- work done and well done. He has found rest! He was indeed a good man. Funeral tomorrow. He was like a father to me.[416]

To those who knew him, it was almost inconceivable that this strong, bold man could be cut down. William Wolfskill, mountain man, intrepid adventurer on the Old Spanish Trail and businessman, was gone but his legacy would live on.

~◞

Personal Observations and Research

As I wrap up my research, I realize that this journey of searching for William Wolfskill has been a daunting as well as an uplifting experience. It has been a genealogical adventure that introduced me to family members whom I never knew existed and encouraged my love of history, taking me down roads across the United States that I would never have seen. Rich and I have stood in empty fields and deserted towns trying to recreate in our minds the westward travels of William as he made his way over the Santa Fe Trail, the Old Spanish Trail and into California. Unearthing my family history has enabled me to meet many others who are on a similar genealogical exploration and connected me to an ever expanding network of people.

Our two children, Chris and Jenny, have also been part of this learning process as they researched and made presentations about William Wolfskill. Our family journey became a detective story that has grown clue by clue and old photo by old photo as we made discoveries about William's life. It has been thrilling to find a new anecdote or piece of research that has not been mentioned anywhere else.

Our search led us to an amazing person who was able to deny death throughout his life when caught in challenging situations that would have decimated a weaker person. It seemed as if William had nine lives and always landed on his feet. But when he grew older, his age and hard life caught up with him. The rifle wound he suffered as a young man in Valverde, New Mexico, plagued him into his old age.

Now that my ten-year journey to find his legacy is nearly complete, I feel that I have found William Wolfskill. Looking at the vast tapestry of his story, I can see that he was a fearless pioneer, loyal friend, brilliant entrepreneur and devoted family man with an enormous heart. Despite the hardships of life, he had accomplished much of what he had set out to do. He had indeed been blessed by his marriage to his lovely wife, Magdalena, his beautiful children by both Magdalena and Luz and his closeness with his brothers. His beloved orchards and vineyards as well as his great success in growing all kinds of fruit from the land were outstanding achievements for a man who had arrived in California with nothing except debt in 1831. One of the civic leaders of Los Angeles, William lived through tumultuous times as the pueblo changed from a small Mexican settlement into an American town after the Mexican-American War. During those transition years, he had served as a bridge between the old California under Mexico and the emerging California under the United States. After all of my research and years dedicated to unraveling William's story, I am honored to be William Wolfskill's and Magdalena Lugo Wolfskill's great-great-granddaughter.

---

400 Newmark, *Sixty Years in Southern California:1853- 1913*, 171.
401 Letter from H.D. Barrows to Timoteo, Los Angeles, July 13, 1864.
402 Letter from Luis Wolfskill, Oakland, October 19, 1865.
403 List of the real and personal property belonging to the Estate of William Wolfskill, deceased, Huntington Collection. Also in summary of "Will of William Wolfskill, June 6, 1866," Thomas Workman Temple.
404 Ibid.
405 Ibid.
406 Ross Miller, "Early Days of City are Described," local Los Angeles newspaper, October 26, 1924.
407 Newmark, *Sixty Years in Southern California:1853- 1913*, 439.
408 List of the real and personal property belonging to the Estate of William Wolfskill, deceased, Huntington Collection. Also in summary of "Will of William Wolfskill, June 6, 1866," Thomas Workman Temple.
408 Ibid.
409 Ibid.
410 Ibid.
411 Summary of "Will of William Wolfskill, June 6, 1866," Thomas Workman Temple.
412 Higbie Wilson, *William Wolfskill: 1798-1866 Frontier Trapper to California Ranchero*, 213.
413 Albert Wilson. *Thompson and West's History of Los Angeles County*, 54.

414   Higbie Wilson, *William Wolfskill: 1798-1866 Frontier Trapper to California Ranchero*, 218. H.D. Barrows, "Diary," September 27, 1866.

415   Letter from Luis to Timoteo, Los Angeles, November 4 1866. Luis wrote that the pain in William's chest "troubled (him) off and on for three weeks before his death. He had it day and night. It did not leave him till a second before his death. He did not eat nor sleep."

416   Higbie Wilson, *William Wolfskill: 1798-1866 Frontier Trapper to California Ranchero*, 218. H.D. Barrows, "Diary," October 3-4, 1866.

LAST CITRUS TREE SAVED FROM WOLFSKILL ORCHARDS

Recognized as the founder of California's commercial citrus industry, William often told people that he planted his first orange grove on the Wolfskill farm in 1841 when Juana Wolfskill, his first child with Magdalena, was born.[417] From that small beginning, the Wolfskill farm grew over the next two decades into a showplace filled with many kinds of citrus including oranges, grapefruit, lemons and limes. By 1862, his orchards were reputed to have two-thirds of the state's orange trees.[418] Joseph Wolfskill, William's son and my great-grandfather, has the distinction of being the first to ship oranges back east in 1877. Joseph sent 300 boxes of oranges from the Wolfskill orchards to St. Louis, Missouri, which took one month by train and cost around $500 in freight charges.[419] The oranges arrived in good condition and opened up the market for California citrus fruit.

Over the years, development slowly chipped away at the orchards as Los Angeles expanded both in population and land size. Drawn to California by its moderate weather and sun, people from all over the country flocked to Southern California causing a boom in land prices during the 1880s. At the same time, a terrible disease, the fluted scale, arrived from Australia that threatened to decimate the orchards.[420] Between those two factors, Joseph eventually sold off the farm. Unfortunately, none of William Wolfskill's orchards are left today except for one lone grapefruit tree located on San Pedro Street in downtown Los Angeles. How this tree survived is a beautiful story about a group of mostly Japanese-American gardeners who saved the last remaining tree of the famous Wolfskill orchards. In 1980, after years of development in the area, this last tree was about to be bulldozed to make way for a parking structure. The Southern California Gardeners' Federation took on the campaign to save the tree and had it brought by crane to its current location at the Japanese-American Cultural and Community Center where it was transplanted.[421] Rich and I have visited the Center many times and always feel a connection back to the Wolfskill orchards. The grapefruit tree still stands and continues to produce grapefruit even though it is over one hundred years old.

Last Citrus Tree Saved from Wolfskill Orchards
Photo by Conchita Thornton Marusich

417 Warner, Hayes, Widney, *An Historical Sketch of Los Angeles County*, 120.
418 Albert Wilson, History of Los Angeles County, 63.
419 Herbert John Webber, Richard Barker and Louise Ferguson, "History and Development of the California Citrus Industry, "*Citrus Production Manual* (University of California Agriculture and Natural Resources, Publication 3539), 6.
420 Newmark, *Sixty Years in Southern California*, 544.
421 Donald R. Hodel, *Exceptional Trees of Los Angeles* (Los Angeles: California Arboretum Foundation, Inc. 1988), 24.

Tips For Genealogists

1. **Start with a passion for finding out information on your ancestor.** My search took over 10 years and was motivated by a profound desire to find out more information about William Wolfskill. Do not get discouraged if the trail of information grows cold. Patience and persistence will win out.

2. **Talk to the oldest relatives in your family.** My mother was my inspiration for this book because she had such a great love of history and pride in our family. I was very fortunate that many of my mother's cousins and descendants of José or Joseph Wolfskill, my great-grandfather, lived to a golden age and were able to share the family history with me. My mother died at 90 years old and two of her first cousins also died in their nineties. They all were very generous with imparting the family history to me.

3. **Ask members of other branches of your family what they know about your common ancestors.** Some of my most helpful information came from cousins who are descendants of William's son, Luis Wolfskill. I didn't know them before I started writing my book, and over the years they have been very supportive.

4. **Always ask family members if they have any old photos, letters, newspaper clippings and scrapbooks about the family.** I found old birth, marriage and death certificates among my mother's papers, and then I ordered the missing certificates online. She also had old scrapbooks that provided a number of the photos in my book.

5. **Consult your local genealogical or historical society for information on your family.** Rich and I always love to visit local genealogy and historical societies whenever possible. The databases can be very helpful, and we have learned so much from community volunteers who usually staff these places. Try to call ahead because these organizations may be run by volunteers and the office hours limited.

6. **The local Mormon Church can also be a great resource since part of their religion is based on researching past family members**. They have wonderful databases that can aid in ancestor research. Rich and I traveled to Salt Lake City, Utah, to do research at their Mormon Family History Center where I found help from local church and community volunteers who always answered my questions with patience and enthusiasm. We were able to find old records both online and on microfilm. One of my relatives from Utah who is a skilled genealogist joined me at the library and helped me navigate through the database. I was so appreciative of her assistance. If you can't travel to Salt Lake, the Church has a network of over 4,745 Family History Centers in 134 countries around the world as of November 2016. These centers offer an opportunity to look through census, birth, death, land and probate records in addition to other historically important documents. There is also free expert phone support at Family Search which offers help 24/7 at 1-866-406-1830.

7. **Talk to the local genealogists, historians and history buffs in the area you are researching.** Many times, we headed to the local historical society, genealogy center or museum and asked who in the community was an expert on the subject matter we were investigating. People were usually helpful and passed along contact information for their local experts.

8. **Be aware that the spelling of our ancestors' last names can vary tremendously.** The Wolfskill name is found in old records as Wolfskill, Wolfscale and Wolfskehl. William was known by many names. He was called William or Guillermo Guisquiel when he was a Los Angeles City Councilmember, William Woolfskill in the 1850 Census and Guillermo Urquides in the marriage book at the Presidio in Santa Barbara, California. The spelling of first names can also vary. William's daughter was known as Magdalena as well as Madalena while his sons had both Spanish and English names. My great-grandfather used the names of José or Joseph Wolfskill interchangeably and his brother was called Luis or Lewis Wolfskill. This can be confusing at first when you are trying to verify a person's identity. Don't forget about nicknames as well, for instance, Martha could be Patsy, Mary could be Molly or Polly, John could be Jack, etc.

9. **Sometimes old documents can be lost through fires, floods, war, earthquakes and other devastation.** During our honeymoon in Yugoslavia in the 1980s, we decided to research some of Rich's ancestors. We started off at the City Hall in Delnice, Croatia, and were told that all the records had been destroyed during the war by the Nazis. Luckily, someone told us that many of the records had been saved by the Catholic Church. We met with the local priest, and when

we told him that we were looking for Rich's ancestors who had left Croatia in the early 20th century, he smiled, left the room for about 10 minutes and returned with several very large leather-bound volumes. As we turned the aging pages with great reverence, he told us how the priests had hidden these volumes from the Nazis and substituted other books which were ultimately destroyed by the Germans. We were able to locate information on Rich's family and found out that his ancestors not only left for America but also for Argentina, which we hope someday to visit and continue our search.

10. **Old census records and city documents can be very helpful.** I've found important information from the Los Angeles City Archives. Aided by the City Archivist, I went through boxes of old documents ranging from the 1836 Los Angeles City Census to the minutes of the City Council meetings in 1844 when William served as a member of the council. Don't forget to check for city directories as they hold a lot of helpful information as well. When checking old records, note the names of your ancestor's neighbors as they could be future spouses or in-laws.

11. **Bibles, Catholic Mass Missals and other religious books/documents can be a great source of information.** My great-grandmother's missal contains a short obituary for Magdalena Lugo Wolfskill from the local newspaper in 1862 with several bits of information which I included in my description of Magdalena's funeral.

12. **Find as much as you can from any writings by your ancestor such as letters, diaries, journals and ledgers.** Also, see what writings can be found of people who experienced an event with the ancestor or who lived during the time of the ancestor. These are called primary sources. Secondary

sources are descriptions based on primary sources. I went back to as many primary sources that I could find about William's life. Even then, it is important to compare primary sources because people can see the same event and have very different recollections of the occurrence.

13. **There are many websites that can be helpful with genealogy research.** The websites that provided me much information include: www.ancestry.com, https://familysearch.org, www.rootsweb.ancestry.com and www.usgenweb.com Many other sites are also excellent in assisting genealogy seekers.

14. **People's names can change over a period of time.** For example, one of the trappers on William's expedition over the Old Spanish Trail was called Ziba Branch. We located one of his descendants in Arroyo Grande, California, close to San Luis Obispo where Ziba settled and owned a large ranch. At first, we were confused since his descendant always called him Francis Branch while we had only heard him referred to as Ziba Branch during William Wolfskill's time. Eventually we realized that we were both talking about the same person. But the different names can lead to confusion.

15. **Libraries, universities, colleges and community colleges can be excellent sources of information about your ancestors.** I was able to find great information and photos at several universities including UC Irvine, UC Davis and UCLA in addition to the Bancroft and the Huntington libraries. Here in Napa, California, our local community college has reference materials that are not found in regular libraries. Saint Helena Library in Napa County is another gem that has an excellent California Collection that contains very difficult-to-find older historical books. Librarians can

be a very important part of your research and can help locate items more efficiently.

16. **Join an organization of similarly minded people who are interested in the same subject matter.** I've become a member of a number of groups such as the Santa Fe Trail Association, Los Pobladores and the Santa Barbara Trust for Historic Preservation. During a recent luncheon for the descendants of the Santa Barbara Presidio, I met many *primos* or cousins who are descendants of the original *Californios* as I am. I also joined the Old Spanish Trail Association (OSTA) in order to understand William's historic journey over the Trail in 1830. I've not only benefitted from their conferences and newsletters but most of all from my interaction with other members who have shared their knowledge. One of the most illuminating experiences occurred when the director of the Southern Utah Chapter of OSTA took Rich and me off-road and showed us the Wolfskill Boulder from 1831 that sits hidden in the forest. When I saw this possible vestige from William's expedition, I felt like I was experiencing history first-hand.

17. **You can gather important information from cemeteries and death records.** An historian in Arrow Rock, Missouri, took us to a long-forgotten Wolfskill cemetery in the middle of an overgrown wooded area in Western Missouri. The cemetery provided an important clue in putting together the Wolfskill story in that it showed us that many Wolfskills had lived in that part of Missouri which encouraged us to keep researching in that area. The website "Find a Grave" is another source that helps people find the graves of their ancestors.

18. **Use the internet to find people, books, museums, associations and all kinds of relevant data.** The internet has

revolutionized research making it so much easier to find information. When I first started my search about William Wolfskill, I mainly went to libraries and looked through stacks of books in archives. But over the past 10 years, so much has been digitized which allows for access through the internet as opposed to traveling to individual libraries. However, reading the actual primary sources from old books and records as much as possible is still the essential part of any research on our ancestors.

19. **Above all, enjoy the process because it is a great experience to put the genealogical pieces of the puzzle together to find an ancestor who is part of us and who walked in such different shoes.**

20. **Since my research on William Wolfskill is an on-going genealogical project, I would greatly appreciate it if people could send me any new information on William, Magdalena and his family that is not in the book. I can be reached at:**

Conchita Thornton Marusich
P.O. Box 3005
Napa, California 94558
USA

I wish you all wonderful adventures as you trace your own family.

BOOKS

Adams, Emma. *To and Fro in Southern California*. 1888. Reprint, New York: Arno Press A New York Times Company, 1976.

Barry, Louise. *The Beginning of the West: Annals of the Kansas Gateway to the American West 1540- 1854*. Topeka: Kansas State Historical Society, 1972.

Blenkinsop, Willis. "A Better Country in Which to Settle: A Biographical Sketch of William Wolfskill." in *The Westerners Brand Book 16*, Edited by Raymund F. Wood Glendale: The Westerners, 1982.

Bryant, Edwin. *What I Saw in California*. 1848. Reprint, Lincoln and London: University of Nebraska Press, 1985.

Buchanan, Rex C. and James R. McCauley. *Roadside Kansas: A Traveler's Guide to Its Geology and Landmarks*. Lawrence, Kansas: University of Kansas, 2010.

Camp, Charles L., ed. *George C. Yount and his Chronicles of the West*. Denver: Old West Publishing Company, 1966.

Carpenter, María Refugio. 1860 Diary, Pleasants Family Papers. Special Collections and Archives, The UC Irvine Libraries, Irvine, California.

Carpenter, María Refugio. 1862 Diary, Pleasants Family Papers. Special Collections and Archives, The UC Irvine Libraries, Irvine, California.

Carter, Harvey L. "Ewing Young." In *Trappers of the Far West.* Edited by Le Roy R. Hafen. 1965. Reprint, Lincoln and London: University of Nebraska Press/First Bison Book Edition, 1983.

Casas, María Raquel. *Married to a Daughter of the Land: Spanish-Mexican Women and Interethnic Marriage in California: 1820-1880.* Reno & Las Vegas: University of Nevada Press, 2007.

Casebier, Dennis G. *Mojave Road Guide: An Adventure Through Time.* Essex, California: Tales of the Mojave Road Publishing Company, 2010.

Cleland, Robert Glass. *The Irvine Ranch of Orange County.* San Marino, California: The Huntington Library, 1952.

Cowan, Robert G. *Ranchos of California: A List of Spanish Concessions 1775-1822 and Mexican Grants 1822-1846* Fresno, California: Academy Library Guild, 1956.

Crampton, C. Gregory and Steven K. Madsen. *In Search of the Spanish Trail: Santa Fe to Los Angeles, 1829-1848.* Salt Lake City: Gibbs-Smith, Publisher, 1994.

De Voto, Bernard, ed. *The Journals of Lewis and Clark*. Boston: The American Heritage Library, Houghton Mifflin Company,1953.

Eisenhower, John S.D. *So Far from God: The U.S. War with Mexico 1846-1848*. Norman: University of Oklahoma Press: 1989.

Estrada, William David. *The Los Angeles Plaza: Sacred and Contested Space*. Austin: University of Texas Press, 2008.

Friesen, Ruth and Steven Heath. Driving the Old Spanish Trail Through Utah and Arizona. Old Spanish Trail, 2015.

Gregg, Josiah. *Commerce of the Prairies*. Edited by Max L. Moorhead. Norman: University of Oklahoma Press, 1954.

Gudde, Erwin G. *1,000 California Place Names: The Origen and Meaning*. Berkeley: University of California Press: 1959.

Guinn, J.M. *A History of California and An Extended History of Los Angeles and Environs*. Volumes 1 and 2. Los Angeles: Historic Record Company, 1915.

Hafen, Leroy R. and Ann W. Hafen. *Old Spanish Trail: Santa Fe to Los Angeles*. Arthur H. Clark Company, 1954. Reprint, University of Nebraska Press, 1993.

Hittell, John S. *Resources in California*. San Francisco: A. Roman and Company: 1867.

Hulbert, Archer Butler., ed. *Southwest on the Turquoise Trail: The First Diaries on the Road to Santa Fe.* Colorado Springs: The Stewart Commission of Colorado College and the Denver Public Library, 1933.

Hayes, Benjamin. *Pioneer Notes.* Los Angeles: Published by Marjorie Tisdale Wolcott, 1929.

Hodel, Donald R. *Exceptional Trees of Los Angeles. Los Angeles*: California Arboretum Foundation, Inc., 1988.

L'Amour, Louis. *The Lonesome Gods.* Toronto, New York, London, Sydney: Bantam Books, 1983.

Mason, William M. *Los Angeles Under the Spanish Flag: Spain's New World.* Burbank, California: Southern California Genealogical Society, Inc., 2004.

McDaniel, Lyn. Ed. *Bicentennial Boonslick History.* Boonslick Historical Society, 1976.

McKittrick, Myrtle M. *Vallejo: Son of California.* Portland, Oregon: Binfords & Mort, Publishers, 1944.

Newhall, Ruth Waldo. *A California Legend: The Newhall Land and Farming Company.* Valencia, California: The Newhall Land and Farming Company, 1992.

Newmark, Harris. *Sixty Years in Southern California: 1853-1913.* Edited by Maurice H. and Marco R. Newmark. 1916. Los Angeles: Dawson's Book Shop, 1984.

Nunis, Doyce. "Milton G Sublette." In *Trappers of the Far West.* Edited by Le Roy R. Hafen Arthur H. Clark. 1965. Reprint, Lincoln and London: University of Nebraska Press/First Bison Book Edition, 1983.

Older, Fremont. *California Missions and their Romances.* New York: Tudor Publishing Co., 1945.

Parmelee, Robert D. *Pioneer Sonoma.* Sonoma: The Sonoma Valley Historical Society: 1972.

Ramsey, Robert W. *Carolina Cradle: Settlement of the Northwest Carolina Frontier, 1747-1762.* Chapel Hill: The University of North Carolina Press, 1964.

Rolle, Andrew F. *California: A History.* New York: Thomas Y Crowell Company, 1963.

Russell, Carl. *Firearms, Traps and Tools of the Mountain Men.* 1967. Albuquerque: University of New Mexico Press, 1977.

Russell, Osborne. *Journal of a Trapper.* Edited by Aubrey L. Haines. 1955. Reprint, Lincoln/London: University of Nebraska Press/First Bison Book Edition, 1965.

Simmons, Marc and Hal Jackson. *Following the Santa Fe Trail: A Guide for Modern Travelers.* Santa Fe, New Mexico: Ancient City Press, 2001.

Starr, Kevin. *California: A History.* New York: The Modern Library, 2005.

Steiner, Harold Austin. *The Old Spanish Trail: Across the Mojave Desert*. Las Vegas, Nevada: The Haldor Company, 1999.

Stephenson, Terry E. *Shadows of Old Saddleback: Tales of the Santa Ana Mountains*. Orange, California: The Rasmussen Press, 1974.

Teiser, Ruth and Catherine Harroun. *Winemaking in California*. New York: McGraw-Hill Book Company, 1983.

Vega, Victoriano. *Vida Californiana 1834-1847*. Bancroft Library: 1877.

Weber, David J. *The Taos Trappers: The Fur Trade in the Far Southwest, 1540-1846*. Norman: University of Oklahoma Press, 1971.

Warner, Colonel J.J., Judge Benjamin Hayes, Dr. J.P. Widney. *An Historical Sketch of Los Angeles County*. Louis Lewin & CO., 1876. Reprint, Los Angeles, California: O.W. Smith, Publisher, 1936.

Wilson, Iris Higbie. *William Wolfskill 1798-1866: Frontier Trapper to California Ranchero*. Glendale: The Arthur H. Clark Company, 1965.

Wilson, John Albert. *Thompson and West's History of Los Angeles County*. 1880. Reproduction, Berkeley, California: Howell-North, 1959.

Wolfskill, William. *Ledger of Accounts 1830-1832*. Photocopy, Huntington Library and Wolfskill Family.

Wolfskill, William. *Ledger of Accounts 1840-1850*. Wolfskill Family.

Wright, Ralph B., ed. *California's Missions*, Los Angeles: California Mission Trails Assn., LTD, 1950.

Yerby, William Edward Wadsworth. *The History of Greensboro, Alabama, From its Earliest Settlement*, Montgomery, Alabama: Paragon Press, 1908.

JOURNAL/MAGAZINE ARTICLES

Barrows, H.D. "A Two Thousand Mile Stage Ride." *Historical Society of Southern California, Los Angeles.* 1896.

Barrows, H.D. "A Pioneer of Sacramento Valley." *Annual Publications of the Historical Society of Southern California of 1897-98-99.* (Volume IV, Read March, 1895): 12-17.

Barrows, H.D. "Reminiscences of Los Angeles in the Fifties and Early Sixties." *Historical Society of Southern California.* (1893): 55-62.

Barrows, H.D "Los Angeles Fifty Years Ago." *Annual Publications, Historical Society of Southern California.* (1905): 203-207.

Barrows, H.D. "William Wolfskill, The Pioneer." *Annual Publications, Historical Society of Southern California.* (1902): 287-294.

Covington, James W. ed. "A Robbery on the Santa Fe Trail 1827," *Kansas Historical Quarterly.* Vol. XXI, No.7, (1955): 560-63. http://www.kshs.org/p/a-robbery-on-the-santa-fe-trail-1827/13109

Day, F.H. "Ziba Branch." *The Hesperian.* Vol. lll, (1859): 337-339.

Guinn, J.M. "The Passing of the Old Pueblo," *Historical Society of Southern California.* (Read December 1901): 113-120.

Lawrence, Eleanor. "On the Old Spanish Trail." *Touring Topics.* (November 1930): 36-39.

"The Foremothers Tell of Olden Times," *The Chronicle*, San Francisco, September 9, 1900. http://www.sfmuseum.org/hist5/foremoms.html

Warner, J.J. "Reminiscences of Early California from 1831 to 1846." *Annual Publications, Historical Society of Southern California.* (1907-1908): 176-193.

Webber, Herbert John, Richard Barker and Louise Ferguson, "History and Development of the California Citrus Industry" in *Citrus Production Manual*, University of California Agriculture and Natural Resources, Publication 3539.

DOCUMENTS/MANUSCRIPTS

Hoffman, Ogden. *Reports of Land Cases Determined in the United States District Court San Francisco.* Numa Hubert, Publisher, 1862.

Kentucky, County Marriages, 1797-1954, database with images, FamilySearch.

Land Grant *Rancho Río de los Putos* Number 232 Northern District (ND), the Bancroft Library, University of California, Berkeley.

Letter of naturalization granted to William Wolfskill by the Taos City Council, Records of the *Ayuntamiento de Taos*.

Letters to Timoteo from the Amy Wolfskill Smith Collection.

1. Letter from William Wolfskill, Los Angeles, May 13, 1861.
2. Letter from Juana Wolfskill, Monterey, February 27, 1862.
3. Letter from H.D. Barrows, Los Angeles, August 26, 1862.
4. Letter from H.D. Barrows, Los Angeles, August 1, 1863.
5. Letter from Joseph Wolfskill, Los Angeles, August 7, 1863.
6. Letter from Manuela Furman, San Francisco, January 29, 1863.
7. Letter signed Joseph Wolfskill, San Francisco, August 3, 1863, perhaps is from Manuela Furman.
8. Letter from Luis Wolfskill, Los Angeles, January 23, 1864.
9. Letter from H.D. Barrows Los Angeles, March 30, 1864.
10. Letter from Luis Wolfskill, Los Angeles, June 12, 1864.
11. Letter from H.D. Barrows, Los Angeles, July 13, 1864.
12. Letter from Francisca Wolfskill, Los Angeles, January 11, 1865.
13. Letter from Joseph Wolfskill, Los Angeles, March 16, 1865.
14. Letter from Luis Wolfskill, San Francisco, March 19, 1865.
15. Letter from Luis Wolfskill, Oakland, October 19, 1865.
16. Letter from Luis Wolfskill, Los Angeles, November 4, 1866.
17. Letter from Victor Furman, San Francisco, April 25, 1867.
18. Letter from Joseph Wolfskill, Los Angeles, January 9, 1868.
19. Letter from Manuela Furman, San Francisco, January 5, 1873.

Los Angeles City Archives:

1. Minutes, January 5, 1844.
2. Register of Los Angeles and its Jurisdiction: Year 1836.

3. Vigilante Execution of Gervacio Alipáz and María del Rosario Villa. Minute Book of the *Ayuntamiento* of the City of Los Angeles, April 7-10, 1836.
4. Session of the *Ayuntamiento*, January 14, 1836.
5. Minutes, January 5, 1844.
6. Minutes, January 12, 1844.

Obituary for Magdalena Lugo Wolfskill. Los Angeles, July 10, 1862.

Permission to William Wolfskill to trap beavers (nutria) on September 2, 1830. Santa Fe Archives, Governor's Letterbook of Communications to officials in New Mexico.

Petition to become a Mexican Citizen by José Guillermo Wolfskill. Mexican Archives of New Mexico.

"Will of William Wolfskill, June 6, 1866," Thomas Workman Temple.

Pleasants Family Papers. Special Collections and Archives, The UC Irvine Libraries, Irvine, California.

1. Pleasants, J.E. "A Mining Trip to Colorado in 1859." Pleasants Family Papers. Unpublished manuscript.
2. Pleasants, J.E. "Los Angeles in 1856." *Touring Topics*. January, 1930.
3. Pleasants, J.E. "Wolfskill Indian Raid." Unpublished manuscript.
4. Pleasants, J.E. "A Fourth of July at San Fernando Mission in 1856." From a handwritten manuscript.

5. Pleasants, J.E. "Tiding Over a Dry Year on the Mojave in 1864." From a handwritten manuscript.
6. Meadows, Frances. "The Diaries of Mary Refugio Carpenter of Los Nietos: 1860-1865." Unpublished manuscript in the Don Meadows Papers.
7. McPherson, William. "Joseph Edward Pleasants." Typed manuscript.

Santa Barbara Mission Archive-Library:

1. Birth document for Magdalena Lugo from Santa Barbara Mission "Año del Señor de 1804" translated "Year of the Lord 1804."
2. Marriage book entry for Magdalena Lugo and William Wolfskill from the Santa Barbara Mission, "Año 1841" (translated "Year 1841") item 233.
3. San Diego Mission, Burials III. Father Holbein officiated at the funeral of Miguel de Pedrorena on April 1, 1850.

The Huntington Library, San Marino, California. The Wolfskill Collection:

1. Letter to John Reid Wolfskill from William Wolfskill, May 30, 1842.
2. Letter to John Reid Wolfskill from William Wolfskill, January 15, 1843.
3. Letter to John Reid Wolfskill from William Wolfskill, June 10, 1843.
4. Letter to John Reid Wolfskill from William Wolfskill, August 7, 1843.

5. Letter to John Reid Wolfskill from William Wolfskill, March 1, 1845.
6. Letter to John Reid Wolfskill from William Wolfskill, January 22, 1847.
7. Letter to John Reid Wolfskill from William Wolfskill, August 10, 1847.
8. Letter to John Reid Wolfskill from William Wolfskill, June 5, 1848.
9. Letter to John Reid Wolfskill from William Wolfskill, October 3, 1848.
10. *Rancho Río de los Putos* Title document recorded in Vol. A, page 369 Records of Benicia, California, August 28, 1849.
11. List of the real and personal property belonging to the Estate of William Wolfskill, deceased.

Wolfskill, Edward or Ned. "A Few of the Things I Remember as Told Me by My Father, the Late J.R. Wolfskill." 1925. Unpublished manuscript. Special Collections, UC Library, UC Davis.

INTERVIEWS/CONVERSATIONS

Elena Wolfskill Thornton, 2003 and 2004.

Victoria Wolfskill Swackenberg. 2003.

Al Matheson, December 27, 2007 and August 16, 2016.

Liz Warren, 2013 and 2014.

Tony Cristler, Assistant Agricultural Superintendent of the Wolfskill Orchards, August 10, 2011.

Ruth Wolfskill Hoelzel, February 2, 2011 and September 5, 2011.

Alice and David Clapsaddle. September 5, 2011 and September 30, 2013.

Joan Hedding, 2016 and 2017.

Cecelia Peña, Descendant of Juan Felipe Peña, on January 10, 2017 and February 4, 2017.

Jeff Trotman, September 26, 2010.

NEWSPAPER ARTICLES

Barrows, H.D. "Wm. Wolfskill, The Pioneer." *Daily Alta California*, San Francisco, (October 12, 1866).

Barrows, H.D. "The Story of an Old Pioneer." *The Wilmington Journal*, Wilmington, (October 20, 1866).

Barrows, H.D. "Wolfskill's Vineyard and Orchard at Los Angeles: The Story of a California Pioneer." *San Francisco Daily Evening Bulletin*, (December 17, 1858).

Missouri Intelligencer, (25 June 1821).

"Winters Express." Reprinted from the *1975 Centennial Edition of the Winters Express*.

"The Story of An Old Trapper," *The San Francisco Bulletin Company*, (October 26, 1866).

STUDIES

Hovius, Matthew. *The Ancestry of Miguel de Pedrorena.* A genealogy study in Spain commissioned by Conchita Thornton Marusich, 2007.

WEBSITES

http://daviswiki.org/putah_creek

http://wc.rootsweb.ancestry.com/cgi-bin/igm.cgi?op=GET&db=mi lliken1&id=I16079 Mike Millikan's website of William Wolfskill's genealogy chart.

http://newmexicohistory.org/places/cimarron-cutoff-of-the-santa-fe-trail

http://oldspanishtrail.org/assets/downloads/trailpersonalityprofile-slover.pdf

http://www.kshs.org/p/a-robbery-on-the-santa-fe-trail-1827/13109

http://www.santafetrailresearch.com/pike/plaza.html

http://www.oldspanishtrail.org/learn/trail_history.php

http://www.huntington.org/information/ecppmain.htm

http://www.schwaldfamily.org

http://ucanr.org/sites/wolfskill2/files/24267.pdf

http://www.sfgenealogy.com/sf/history/hgpop.htm

http://openjurist.org/59/us/556/the-united-states-v-juan-manuel-vaca-and-juan-felipe-Peña

http://www.oac.cdlib.org/findaid/ark:/13030/kt6v19r84r/entire_text/
http://www.oac.cdlib.org/findaid/ark:/13030/tf967nb619/

http://pamelastorm.com/wlf_a.htm

http://www.adabi.org.mx/content/descargas/inventarios/220_concordia_sin.pdf

http://historia.uasnet.mx/maestria/archivos/tesis/15/tesis%20francisco%20osuna.pdf

http://www.arboretum.org/explore/our-history/

INDEX

Made in the USA
Middletown, DE
10 October 2023

40589779R00146